Ms. Pinchpenny's
Book of
Interior Design

Dorothy Parker is the author of

The Wonderful World of Yogurt

Feeling Fine, Looking Great

Home Preserving Made Easy (with Vera Gewanter)

Ms. Pinchpenny's Book of Kitchen Management

She has contributed to and written introductions for
*The Great Cooks' Guide to Ice Cream and Other Frozen
    Desserts*
The Great Cooks' Guide to Rice Cooking
The Great Cooks' Guide to Cookies

Ms. Pinchpenny's Book of Interior Design

by Dorothy Parker

 VAN NOSTRAND REINHOLD COMPANY
New York • Cincinnati • Toronto • London • Melbourne

Illustrations by Ray Skibinski

Copyright © 1979 by Dorothy Parker
Library of Congress Catalog Card Number 78-17732
ISBN 0-442-26558-1

Published in 1979 by Van Nostrand Reinhold Company
A division of Litton Educational Publishing, Inc.
135 West 50th Street, New York, NY 10020, U.S.A.

Van Nostrand Reinhold Limited
1410 Birchmount Road
Scarborough, Ontario M1P 2E7, Canada

Van Nostrand Reinhold Australia Pty. Ltd.
17 Queen Street
Mitcham, Victoria 3132, Australia

Van Nostrand Reinhold Company Limited
Molly Millars Lane
Wokingham, Berkshire, England

16 15 14 13 12 11 10 9 8 7 6 5 4 3 2 1

Library of Congress Cataloging in Publication Data

Parker, Dorothy, 1922-
    Ms. Pinchpenny's book of interior design.

    Includes index.
    1. Interior decoration—Handbooks, manuals, etc.
I. Title.
NK2115.P287   747   78-17732
ISBN 0-442-26558-1

Contents

Introduction

The Penny-Pincher Philosopher of Decoration embraces three main tenets: first, in making a home out of a house (or an apartment) always go for comfort and livability; second, never buy anything that you can make, steal, beg, inherit, or just plain find for free; and third, avoid like the plague the conventions, principles, and trends of the A.S.I.D.

In case that acronym means nothing to you, those letters are the initials of the American Society of Interior Designers. This august group, like parents and gods, has ways of making laymen feel very guilty if, for example, we don't get the living room walls painted in decorator colors (whatever they happen to be this year) or cleave to the only shape permissible for lamp bases and shades (ginger-jar form seems to be "in" this year, and, for the shade, accordian-pleated, white parchment—any other combination simply will not do). Now, you know and I know that in the realm of haute couture nothing is deader than last season's fashions; this is equally true of trends in decorating. There is no more self-evident truism than that last year's "in" is this year's "out."

Moreover, to hire a professional to do over a room just naturally goes against the grain of the economy-minded home manager of taste and discrimination, who really *does* know better than any interior designer what he or she likes in the way of furniture, furnishings, decoration, and ambiance. Trust your own innate good sense and your independent nature. Don't be dictated to on the question of what *things* you want to live with, any more than you would let someone else choose the person or persons with whom you will share your home. They're your living quarters, not a decorator's; what suits him or her won't necessarily make your abode a thing of beauty

1

and a joy forever. It has always struck me as an obvious truth that the person who is going to live in a home is the best judge of how it should be furnished. The flats or cottages that get my vote for the ones I-would-most-like-to-be-marooned-on-a-desert-isle-with always have been furnished and decorated by their occupants.

Lord knows it's difficult enough for two people of very distinct opinions and divergent tastes, who are going to occupy the same premises, to arrive at a modus vivendi as to how a room should be dressed and maintained. My husband, for instance, belongs to the "hold down the corner" school of furniture placement, while I delight in expanses of bare floor and empty wall; he is an inveterate squarer-away, whereas I take considerable pleasure in asymmetry. It takes some compromising to get our living space into a shape and arrangement we both feel comfortable with. How could we possibly expect even the most dedicated and inventive interior designer to be able to please all three of us?

It's very risky, in fact, to make *any* decoration decisions on behalf of someone else, even with the best will in the world and some money to spend—a lesson I learned at a very early age. My older sister had gone away to counsel in summer camp after high school graduation, an opportunity that my sainted mother seized to "do over" my sister's bedroom. Dragging me along, that good woman pored over wallpaper sample books, paint chips, and fabric swatches for days until she found just the right combination of pastels, flowers, ruffles, and flounces that seemed to her to effect the proper transformation. Those pinks and blues and organdies and chintzes made Big Sister's sleeping and studying quarters just the right sort of place for someone about to matriculate in college, try on dancing dresses, fall in love, and all manner of other feminine joys. When my sister returned home at summer's end, we all gathered around to witness her surprise and delight at the changes that had been wrought—and found ourselves cowering before her rage and indignation. How had we *dared* imagine we could guess her taste and preferences? Where was her comfortable, worn-out armchair, her chipped goosenecked study lamp, all the squirrel skins, horses' tails, birds' nests, and other "stuff" she used to have pinned to the walls? To her filial credit (and my mother's and my relief) she soon made peace with her homecoming gift, largely because we had had the prudence and good sense not to burn the decaying hides and other assorted junk, which were soon returned to their rightful places on the pastel wallpaper and the gossamer shag rug. Restoration of familiar objects took place and peace reigned once more. But, from that time to this, I've never presumed I could guess what furnishings are just right for someone else. I can only make suggestions as to how to save money on them.

To return to the primary guiding principle, I can't stress hard enough the comfort and livability angle. If you're not supremely comfortable in your own home, where can you be? That's where you let down your hair, take off your shoes, sprawl, slump, scratch, whistle while you work. A graceful, but fragile, little Victorian (or Empire or Louis Quatorze) straight chair may please the eye with its lines and excite the imagination with its coloring; but if you weigh over 100 pounds and, in an excess of good spirits, lean back in it, you'll find yourself on the floor and your side chair in two pieces. (This happened before my eyes to my beloved Uncle Percy one Thanksgiving Day in the early thirties. That disaster, as much as the fact that the Great Depression was upon us, was the genesis of my future propensity for furnishing *my* homes from the town dump.) Chairs that can't be sat upon are not only a hazard to life and limb, but a contradiction in terms, as well, as are beds that don't promote sleep, floor coverings that *dare* you to walk on them, and tables whose surfaces can't support objects wet or dry, hot or cold, stationary or movable.

Only recently I finally divested myself of a drop leaf, gateleg cherry-wood table. Years ago, upon moving for the first time into an apartment of more than two rooms, I had sunk a small fortune into that table. Though its high-gloss surface remained unmarred and handsome, I had hated that table for the better part of a quarter-century. Such was its construction that there was no way for any number of people greater than one to sit at it. Had I possessed the foresight to try out that table in all its positions, envisioning various numbers of diners, I never would have made that mistake in the first place. (Lady who bought it at my garage sale, forgive me. I hope you're using that damned table in the parlor with its sides down, not in the dining room.) The virtues of the lowly table I now dine off will be extolled in Chapter 2. Chief among these virtues is that it was free.

Optimum utility and esthetically pleasing appearance are not the sole province of the Early American style in furniture, though those Yankee pioneers had some really good ideas that have stood the test of time admirably. Some contemporary items of many nationalities and various materials have the simplicity of line plus awareness of the contours of the human body that promote comfort and usefulness, while committing no assault to the eye or other nerve centers. Study furniture in magazine and newpaper ads and feature stories, in catalogs and store displays, and in the rooms that really work in homes you visit before you go out and plunk down any hard-earned cash on a purchase of a major piece. And, of course, comparison-shop until your legs buckle.

I've just heard on the radio about something called a "Buying Service"—not a decorator, but more like a food co-op—that can get you furniture at wholesale prices. It is said to be listed in the *Yellow Pages* of the phone directory. This may be a feature of large cities only; but it may not. I'd appreciate any small-city dwellers looking it up and letting me know.

If you postpone the acquisition of a major piece long enough, you may find you don't really need or want that particular one. Or you may have *found* it, thrown out by your neighbor on trash collection day, or dumped by him in the town landfill area, he having decided to let a decorator revise his family room and recreate his life-style. If you've developed a good scavenger's eye, you may have spied it abandoned on the sidewalk you traverse on the way to work or in the incinerator room where you dispose of your garbage. Make a point of snatching it up quickly, even if you have to collar a colleague or pay the super to help you, because it won't be there when you next pass that way: it will be installed in someone else's home. Don't be dismayed if your new-found treasure is not the color, finish, or covering that will harmonize with your existing scheme. These characteristics can be changed so easily and so inexpensively. If one part is missing, it may not be all that vital or irreplaceable. Amazing the propensity of Americans for discarding the odd, completely mouse-free, overstuffed chair, for example, because it has somehow lost one of its 4-inch legs. Legs don't need to match exactly if they are covered by a skirt and don't show; legs need only to be sturdy and roughly equal in length.

Serendipity is one of the marvelous aspects of serious scavenging. You just never know when you're going to come upon that cobalt blue cocktail shaker that the discarder didn't realize was Depression Glass (and could have sold to a dealer for a price four times its original value) while actually you're searching for a thrown-away rusty tin tray or box to paint tole style. Very often you will find (or be given by a friend moving his home) the very object you've been planning to make or buy. It's like learning a new word and then falling over it in everything you read or hear. An increased awareness of the thing you covet turns it up for you, or enhances the X-ray quality of your scavenger's eye; you *know* under just which pile of last week's newspapers it lies or at which garage sale advertised for this coming Sunday in the local crier it can be found. For the latter circumstance, by the way, get there at opening time, zero in on your "thing," then offer half the price on the tag. In most cases, you'll get it. Tag sale operators are no more immune to the early, quick unloading than are secondhand shop proprietors. Presto! You own that wrought-iron rolling tea wagon that will serve so many purposes in your living/dining room area. Multifunctional objects are, of course, a must for the occupant of a tiny house or miniscule apartment, but more about that in Chapter 9.

I've spoken a bit about the scavenger's gimlet eye. Since I am equipped with two, I know whereof I speak. It's impossible to keep these orbs from swiveling from side to side and up and down—to cover all contingencies—while walking the sidewalks of cities. Most disruptive if you're trying to carry on intelligent conversation with your companion at the same time. Oh well, you can't have everything, and the next thing you must develop to go with your clever eyes is a thick hide. You can't be sensitive to the "slings and arrows" or feel hurt if a passerby looks askance at your rooting around in garbage or removing the top layer of trash to discover the jewels concealed beneath. Your benefactors, the disposers of marvelous junque, very seldom work on the same priority system as you. The best finds are not always on top!

The penny-pinching decorator must take advantage of imperfection, wherever he finds it. A crack in a plaster wall or ceiling is inviting you to cover that surface with wallpaper, fabric, or that Navajo or Oriental rug that Aunt Tillie left you in her will. If the floorboards in your new home are rotted in one spot, rather than laying down a complete new floor, cut out the offending members and sink into the floor a window box, or plastic or metal trough. Use it as a planter or to hold some handsome stones and shells you've collected. If your bedroom windows (as is often the case in ranch houses) are too high and small, why not curtain them and make a headboard too in one fell swoop by covering a tall wooden frame with some loose, light fabric? (Directions for this and other headboards in Chapter 3.) If a huge living room and a tiny bedroom is your ideal and the opposite is what your new flat consists of, what's the matter with turning the small living room into the boudoir and letting the mammoth bedroom become the living room? I knew an apartment dweller in Greenwich Village who did just that. The only disadvantage was that you entered the apartment through the bedroom—a small price to pay for locating the sleeping place in the quietest room in the house. More about imperfections and their utilization in ensuing chapters.

This can hardly be deemed imperfection—it's more like an embarrassment of riches—but allow me one more room-switch story. Some people I know recently moved into a six-room house with a full bath both upstairs and downstairs. In time, they found they never used the downstairs bathtub and hardly ever the washbasin in that room, which was close to the kitchen. On my ingenious advice, they covered the bathtub with a plywood slab topped with foam rubber in a canvas envelope, scattered some soft pillows against the surrounding tile, and lo and behold, downstairs bathroom became the TV room. The tube now occupies the formica-topped cabinet into which the sink is sunk, conveniently placed directly across the room from the ex-bathtub, and the toilet is disguised with a large, potted plant—a perfect solution to the problem of plenty.

Another axiom in the penny-pincher philosophy of beauty is to let the unexpected play a part in your decoration. Or else, you may have a completely functional living space that looks like everyone else's, doesn't express your individuality, and blends into the woodwork, so to speak. It will be a great bore. What price comfortable quarters if it's tedious to look at them. If you furnish your home out of the garbage cans, this is not usually a looming danger. But sometimes even the scavenger or do-it-yourselfer lacks imagination in his decoration. He uses everthing he finds or makes precisely as it's intended. By this, I'm not plumping for making a lamp base out of the coffee grinder you found in the junk shop or employing the splendid old oxen yoke you dug up out of the grown-over meadow as a garage front ornament or gate in your rail fence. These "conversions" are just other forms of hackneyed triteness. But the oxen yoke, carried back to a city apartment and fastened over a window to loop a curtain through, or used as a towel rack in kitchen or bath—that's nutty enough to be noticed. So is the wooden coffee grinder with its bottom fastened to a bedroom wall, its iron handle and bowl used to hang a colorful dressing gown or bathrobe on. A hand-hooked semicircular "Welcome" rug just inside the front entrance door is yawn-worthy; use it instead as a bath mat, by bedside, or in front of a closet door. One of the most interesting, purely decorative objects in an over-decorated house I lived in for a time was a policeman's leather pistol holster hung on the wall with a spray of paper flowers blooming out of it—truly an incongruity and a conversation-piece in the best sense of the word.

If you want to become an amateur interior designer on a tight budget, loosen up your notion of what things are *for*. Look at them with a liberated eye and you'll begin to see all sorts of possibilities. Inside a discarded ironing board is a plant holder trying to get out, whereas a bow-legged wicker fern stand found in your mother's attic may be just the thing for that sunless corner of your study where you'd like to stow some records, books, magazines, or your bargello or crocheting. Correct the fractured wooden leg by gluing, bolstering with a metal rod and some wire, or replacing with a spare broomstick. Inherent in the rubberized dish drainer is the capacity for hanging up neckties, belts, or scarves, for storing rolled-up socks, for drying just-cooked lasagna noodles, for stand-up folder files, and a hundred other uses.

It isn't only "found objects" of ancient vintage or rigid form that can be used in unexpected ways. The inspired penny pincher stares long and hard at fabrics and other flat dry goods that have already lived long lives and are about to be pitched into the trash bin. See what they might *become*. Those drapes, if reversed to minimize their fading, might become a bedspread, and vice versa. That aged tablecloth has doubtless achieved the proper softness to be turned into pillowcases or a mattress cover for the baby's crib or carriage. Those three-year-old bath mats that make your lavatory look like Tobacco Road won't do so if you turn them inside out and use them to cover the foam rubber seat and backrest for the wooden-frame chair you found abandoned on County Road.

Things you've worn can costume your rooms when you've tired of them as clothing; textiles that have clothed your furniture can, with a little flick of the wrist, be turned into togs. A heavy, warm pants suit given me by a friend opting for tropical climes has made a dandy hassock covering; one of my most opulent-looking armchairs is upholstered in what was a corduroy evening skirt. This was a "learning experience" that turned out so successful that it's been the principal chair in my series of living rooms of the last few years. A length of burnt orange cotton twill has been a cape, a pillow sham, a blouse, and, finally, a collection of pot holders—according to my circumstances of interior and condition of wardrobe. Army blankets left over from summer camp days have draped a wall to provide a perfect baffle for stereo sound. My favorite dress from high school days was something I whipped up from a green-and-white candlewick dressing-table skirt. And where would the fashion industry be without pillow ticking and other fabrics once deemed appropriate only for covering mattresses and sleeping pillows? But that's another book. . . .

This book is written to help you achieve a cozy, comfortable nest or a sublimely elegant apartment that lives and works *with* you, not *against* you, without depleting your bank account or ruining your nerves. Don't you just love those newspaper articles entitled something like "How We Over-Furnished Ten Rooms for Seventy-Nine Dollars and Forty Cents"? When you read on, you find that the wife just happens to be a cousin of W. and J. Sloane and a sister of Billy Baldwin, and the husband just chanced to bring with him a forty-nine-piece sterling silver service and a nice old carved wood chest that had been in his family since Marco Polo brought it from China to Venice? No, nothing like that. Just good, sensible advice about household things and how to acquire them at little or no cost.

Because I can't think of a better way to organize this gold mine of information, I'll do it by rooms. I'll start with the one without which most people—and dogs and cats—can't stay alive: the heart of the home, the kitchen.

Dorothy Parker
Bridgewater, Connecticut

1

Cooking Room

The kitchen, be it a tiny compact work space in a studio apartment or a huge, cavernous Victorian room that clearly anticipates a host of servants marching around it, can't help but become the heart of your home. As such a vital nerve center, it should command first consideration when you start thinking about decorating—or redecorating. A good deal of time is spent in the cooking room by *some*one—conservative estimates say 30 percent of the average homemaker's day—so it should be a good-looking, comfortable, cheerful, light, airy room, if you can possibly manage it.

There are people all over the country who make their livings by replanning badly designed kitchens. (Architects who never cook should leave that part of the planning of homes to someone who does, and the smart ones *do* consult home economists or other food authorities.) But you can do it yourself with ease by going through the motions of preparing a dinner: think out a menu and then walk through all the steps. Prepare it, get it on the table, and then clean it up afterwards. In this sort of "dry run," it will become evident to you which appliances or articles of furniture are badly placed. Simplistically speaking, sink, stove, and refrigerator should mark the three corners of a triangle walked by a meal-getter, with preparation counters in between. Perhaps, with the work of plumbers, electricians, or cabinetmakers, you can switch the locations of your appliances at minimal cost. Sometimes the simple rehanging of a door on the refrigerator, dish cabinet, broom closet, or oven, so that it opens from left to right rather than right to left, can work wonders in facilitating meal-getting.

As for cabinets, it's possible that your thinking is a generation or two behind the times. In these days of the "let-it-all-hang-out" school of decoration, open shelves are far more to the point. Besides, cooking utensils are such fascinating-looking objects that they themselves constitute "decoration." If you have a handsome group of pots and pans, it's a pity to hide them behind closed doors. Your flame red (or peacock turquoise or butter yellow) enameled Dutch oven can be a focal point for your room, plus an important key to build the color scheme around. Blue-and-white spatter enamel cookware, which was declassé for some years, has come into its own again and is now providing the keynote for many modern kitchens.

Remember when all kitchen appliances *had* to be white? There just wasn't any other color a kitchen was allowed to be? My mother had the first lime green refrigerator ever known in the suburban Massachusetts town where I grew up. It was a small-town scandal. Actually, the only reason it wasn't dead white was that it was a secondhand monstrosity which we painted green to cover up the scratches in its finish and to match the wall it was to be placed against; we wanted it to recede a bit and not stand out like a sore thumb. Today there are no holds barred in the colors of stoves, refrigerators, dishwashers, and even kitchen sinks—avocado seems popular just now—and most of these hues are a lot easier to keep clean than antiseptic (and fingerprint-collecting) white.

If you are about to color your kitchen cheerful, consider the following schemes:

avocado appliances, chocolate brown walls, red and orange accents;

copper brown appliances, off-white woodwork, vinyl wallpaper of purple, yellow, and green plaid;

burnt umber appliances, deep-blue enameled walls and ceiling, blonde walnut shelves and trim;

stainless steel appliances and countertops, warm red tiled floor, canary yellow walls and ceiling.

Wallpapering kitchens, once a no-no, is now not only a yes-yes, but a thing thousands of kitchen owners who once considered themselves "all thumbs" have done. (If you don't actually own the kitchen, ask the landlord if you can take the cost of the materials and your labor off the next month's rent.) In some kitchens the greatest challenge is measuring the space to be covered—especially if it's all chopped up with windows, doors, hung cabinets or shelves, and the like—and deciding on the width and number of wallpaper rolls. The first time out you may want to work with a prepasted covering. All you have to do, after cutting it to size and shape, is dip it in a sinkful of water and smooth it on with a damp rag. Easy as pie. Choose a simple pattern, not one with a fraction-of-an-inch matching problem. Next time you can graduate to a wall covering that has to have glue applied to its back (these are somewhat less expensive) and requires fastidious overlapping and joining.

The first kitchen wallpapering job I did was to apply a wheat-colored tweedy vinyl right over the existing wallpaper, a tiny, French-Provincial-looking print paper that busied up the small room to within an inch of its life. That's the way to do it, especially on aged plaster walls. The paper that's there may be the only thing holding the old plaster together. If, on the other hand, papering is not your bag *and* you have confidence in the solidity and strength of the basic wall material, scrape the old paper off before you do your wall painting. For kitchens be sure you have a hard-finish, washable paint, or else every time you scrub around the stove you'll remove part of your paint job. Latex (rubber-based) paints are good; so are non-rubber, oil-based enamels in shiny or flat finishes. If your kitchen range has a hood, don't overlook the hood when you are redecorating. You can paint the hood, naturally, but you can also wallpaper it (because of its shape, cut out a pattern that fits it first from newspaper), just as you can wallpaper other nonwall surfaces in the kitchen—refrigerator or cabinet doors, for instance, or the fronts of drawers. With any curved surface it is especially important to experiment with a paper pattern first.

Don't make the mistake of a friend of mine who decided that gluing fabric to the walls would give his city-slicker kitchen that desirable rough "country" look. The only fabric his budget could allow (or so he thought) was burlap. Now burlap walls are not only sensible and cheap to come by, but are very attractive and appropriate—in some locations. (You can even buy burlap all fixed up with adhesive backing.) In a poorly ventilated kitchen, however, next to the cooking surface of a person whose principal method of cooking is to stir-fry, it breeds disaster! Those rough burlap fibers absorbed and hung onto every atom of grease that arose into the air, and there was *no way* to clean the walls. If he had bought instead fabric-backed vinyl with the *look* of burlap, he'd have been poorer, but cleaner.

Once, while converting an old Chelsea brownstone rooming house to a private home, I removed dozens of layers of wallpaper from a back room used as a bedroom. When I got down to the venerable plaster, I accidentally removed some of that, too, and discovered a good brick wall. So it was off with the rest of the crumbling plaster, and one wall of the room was that marvelous play of earth colors displayed by weathered brick. I converted that room into the kitchen.

Other good kitchen wall coverings to think about are:

simulated brickwork (a plastic wall covering);

rough-cut wood paneling;

shingles;

book jackets or magazine covers pasted on and then varnished over.

Washability is, of course, the keynote. Keep it in mind when choosing wall and ceiling coverings, surfaces on which you'll prepare food, and floor coverings. Exposed, random-width floorboards are peachy in big country kitchens, and stay-flat rag rugs can protect that oak or pine wood near stove and sink (see page 119 for instructions on how to make some out of nothing), but in the small city kitchen there's still nothing like linoleum, asphalt tile, or one of their relatives. If you are laying it yourself, invest in a cushiony underpinning if the flooring material doesn't come with one attached. This will pay off tremendously in comfort for you and gratitude from your downstairs neighbor. Handsome as some solids and geometric patterns in flooring are, you will find that a mottled pattern is easy on the nerves, combines well with the rest of the decoration, and doesn't need washing and waxing as often. (Many kitchen floor coverings never need waxing at all and they are surprisingly only a little bit higher in cost than the old-style linoleum.) If you come by more than you need at a bargain rate, grab it. You can use some up on the floors of closets and cabinets or on the wall near the sink and stove.

Formica-covered work surfaces seem to be a plus as far as realtors are concerned these days, but they don't cut much ice with me, fresh from a house whose kitchen was filled with butcher-block-imitation formica. You can't put a very hot pot from the front burner down on formica. If you are cursed with formica on everything, I suggest that you surround the range top with a hot-pot surface made from one of the following materials:

ceramic tile—just lay it on top of the unsatisfactory surface or glue it down with an epoxy glue;

metal grillwork trivet—something picked up in a dump or junk
shop;

a stout oak plank—glue bits of rubber mat to its underside.

Real brickwork in the kitchen is a nice touch with a warm, informal look to it. If you happen to be a brick mason, that is one way to
come by a handsome, durable work surface next to your range top.
But if you are not so blessed, see if you can pick up a few discarded
bricks from a backyard or building site and make a hot-pot surface
near your stove. Arrange them in a square or oblong shape and tie
them in place with a rope or old belt or glue them together with
white or epoxy glue. Either solid bricks or those with holes through
them will do.

Real bricks or masonry building-blocks have a hundred decorative and functional uses around the house; never pass them by if you
can possibly carry them home. After you've built a hot surface with
them, you can build other things, such as "steps" for your herbs and
spices to be arranged on, either in the open or behind a cabinet door,
or a spice rack as specified on page 24.

Real honest-to-goodness butcher blocks are terribly chic now,
and, hence, very costly. Whether it is one of those solid, chunky,
heavy tables with slots on the side for hanging cleavers in or a building material you get at the lumberyard, a butcher-block-topped table
or dishwasher or cabinet or "island" is an expensive proposition.
You can sometimes get around the prohibitive cost by picking such
a piece of furniture up at a secondhand store or auction. They aren't
usually *antiques* and, hence, are not priced quite as high as the eighteenth-century cherry highboy. Butcher block as a cabinet topping,
chopping board, or whatever, can be a most satisfying part of your

kitchen's decor. Clean it every week or so by scrubbing with hot water and a touch of baking soda or lemon juice.

If you are lucky enough to acquire at an auction (or as a friend of mine did, at an art-supply shop that was going out of business) one of those very sturdy, early-twentieth-century, rectangular wooden tables with Doric-column legs and a low shelf underneath, you have an important piece for any room large enough to accommodate it. If the middle top surface is marred by years of service, consider putting the table in your large country kitchen and sinking the burners from your soon-to-be-replaced range into the tabletop. I saw such a table "done" this way in a converted barn; it was a smashing piece of inspired skullery decoration. The oven, of course, was in the wall.

If your kitchen boasts a window, lucky you; if several, luckier still, especially if they are arranged in such a way as to provide cross ventilation and there is no ventilator hood over the stove. With only one window (and no built-in ventilator) the first way to "decorate" the window should be to add a ventilating fan. Make room for that first; then you can think about what else goes with the window. If the window is not needed for light or view, a witty way to handle it would be to paint a design that suggests the contours of the ventilating fan right on the glass.

or make a "stained glass" window with decals;

or cover the glass sections with designs, such as vegetables, fruits, stars, stripes, geometric forms, cut out of contact paper;

or put shelves of glass or wood on which you can store cans and boxes of foodstuffs or tableware across the window;

or make the window part of the wall around it by simply painting it, glass plus wood or metal, the same color.

Plant pots full of herbs in the kitchen window are pretty, appropriate, and useful. Have you thought of a pot planted with cherry tomatoes or tiny cucumbers or a tray of lettuce on the windowsill? Growing your salad in the window is fitting even for a small city apartment and just as fine a "decoration" as hanging ferns.

The first thing I do upon moving into a new kitchen is to take down any curtains (cafe or other) or blinds (venetian or other) or shades that may be hung there. Natural light is just as important in the cooking room as any other. But if curtains are your thing, remember that checked gingham is not the only material appropriate to the

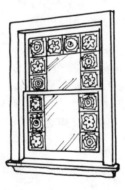

kitchen. Make kitchen curtains of any easily cleanable material, such as:

terry cloth or other toweling;

bed sheets or any close-woven cotton;

old shower curtains that have outlived their usefulness in the bathroom;

fabric or plastic chair webbing, sewn together into "lengths" or simply tacked across window, from top to bottom or side to side;

light canvas or sailcloth;

old, faded denim blue jeans, pockets and all (you can put hot-
   pot holders in the pockets);
bandana cloth, blue or red.
   A particularly effective treatment for kitchen windows is to leave
them clear and blank and uncurtained and to decorate *around* them
instead. Frame the glass and the light that comes through it with a
border. Paint, paper, decal, or stencil a frame around the window,
especially if there's a color or pattern you want to carry across the
room to tie it together. A window framed in a row of tiles like the
tiles around your cooking area or adhesive-backed paper in a tile
design add coherence to the room. Strips of aluminum foil can border a window in an easily cleanable way; strips of cork or pegboard
have a good, "kitcheny" look, plus they provide a place where you
can hang up implements or tack up a recipe or marketing list.
   I happen to like matchstick roll-up blinds in a kitchen. That's
probably because I'm partial to matchstick blinds and like them
anywhere and everywhere. See Chapter 8 for more window ideas
and see if they apply to your kitchen windows.
   So many cooking utensils are of such interesting shapes that they
make good wall hangings for your kitchen. Besides, if you suspend
them from cup-hooks underneath a low shelf or from a corkboard
or pegboard wall close to your preparation and cooking surfaces,
you will find that they are out of the way, yet handy for grabbing.
It's much better than rummaging through the back of a narrow

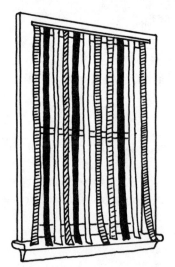
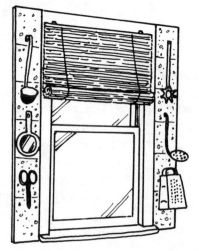

drawer in the middle of soufflé making. Picture a garlic press, a four-sided aluminum grater, an orange squeezer, an egg beater, and one of those harplike boiled-egg slicers. Tongs and whisks and slotted spoons are fun to look at; the wooden variety of these tools make appropriate kitchen window hangings—or wall decorations, if you can resist cooking with them. If your wooden cooking utensils are in constant use, they can still "decorate" your kitchen by living in decorative mugs at stove side.

Strainers and colanders in various materials and sizes are useful and decorative, too. Most of the trendy kitchens I know now include one of those triple hanging wire baskets on chains for holding root vegetables, etc. An element of surprise can be introduced by filling one of the baskets with potted plants instead. Gleaming copper skillets, crepe pans, pots, and bowls are dandy items to "dress up" the kitchen, as are enameled aluminum or iron utensils that mix or match colors. Trivets, whether of scrollwork wrought iron in the Early American mode or handmade straw in Contemporary Woolworth's, are ideal as hot plates and as wall hangings, too.

If there is a good deal of open wall space in your kitchen, here is a nifty decorating idea. Paint the walls gleaming white and fill them with hooks for hanging utensils. Paint black lines around the hanging pots, pans, and other tools of the trade. Besides providing cues for guest cooks and bottle washers they make a marvelous design element. Now carry this black-and-white motif throughout the room: white ceiling, big black wood-burning stove, black-and-white checkered flooring, stripes of black and white at windows (either window shades or curtains). Splash nearly every rainbow color around the room as the accents—hot-pot holders, kettles and pots, hanging plants, candles in candlesticks. In the center of the room I see a beaten-up trestle table or one made of a plank set on sawhorses, covered with a piece of shiny black oilcloth. The oilcloth is simply tacked in place on the underside of the tabletop. This table doubles as food-preparation "island" and casual-meals surface; when neither of these functions is called for decorate it with a large white ironstone bowl or a cornucopia of colorful nuts, fruits, or vegetables of the season.

Of course, the kitchen is the room where foodstuffs help do your decorating. Matching glass jars filled with nuts, seeds, or pasta in various shapes make charming decoration, as do onions, garlic, or shallots twisted together in a hanging column or bunched together in the plastic mesh bags they were bought in. These bags, incidentally, make excellent dirty-pot scrapers, too. Find glass jars at the glass recycling center or save them from your purchases of peanut butter, honey, pickles, or whatever. What sight is better than a large wooden bowl full of fresh fruit and vegetable mixtures? Bananas, apples, and eggplant are frequent color contrasts in my bowls. But how about purple grapes, lemons, and potatoes; zucchini, mangoes, and walnuts; artichokes, oranges, acorn squash, and a cucumber; a fresh pineapple surrounded with plums and grapefruit? By the way, when you have eaten the pineapple, remove the top intact, put its bottom into water until it grows some roots, and then plant it for your very own homegrown kitchen cactus plant.

The "large wooden bowl" mentioned above costs far more than it should if bought new. But "rejects" at factory outlets or cut-rate shops are a bargain. These bowls, unloved by the department-store or gift-shop buyer, are often more interesting in form, grain, or finish than the first-run bowls. A small one, which I picked up for pennies in Vermont, together with a wooden gavel left over from when I was the presiding officer of something or other, is my mortar and pestle. (The sister bowls are individual salad servers.)

Three frying pans that I found in the town dump now decorate one wall of my kitchen. They weren't worth resurfacing for cooking, but the two small copper-bottomed ones and the one medium-sized one in robin's-egg blue enamel are perfect accompaniments for the useful and lovely baskets hanging there. All of the baskets were free: one was rescued from a city incinerator room, one was a Christmas gift, which was filled with edible goodies—the best kind of holiday offering—and the last had been discarded in the town dump along with a wad of green Easter-egg-nest paper.

Wicker, wood, enamelware, and metal—these are all materials that make beautiful and functional objects for a kitchen. In all the cooking rooms I've lived in there's never been quite enough space for all the cooking and eating tools I'd like to have around; or, rather, there *wasn't* until I discovered two important principles. First, there is an abundance of space to be utilized in the upper half of most kitchens that is frequently overlooked (underlooked?). A lighting fixture or a skylight is not the only thing that can occupy the ceiling. Try a shelf of light materials over your food preparation table or counter; a rectangle of balsa wood suspended from the ceiling with two metal brackets on each side; or one of those skyhooks called "pot hangers," which are wrought-iron hoops with S-shaped hooks for holding pots and pans and all manner of paraphernalia. These useful contraptions provide a very French look. And they needn't, by the way, be bought in the gourmet cooks' corner of your local department store at highway-robbery prices. I saw a sizable one recently in a hardware shop for 26 dollars. A small semicircular one for a wall can be had for between 4 and 5 dollars.

But how about fashioning one for yourself out of some material other than wrought iron, which just conceivably may pull down your old ceiling? Here are some notions:

a hollow aluminum curtain rod, held aloft by hooks screwed into the ceiling and fitted out with bits of chain with curved metal hooks on their bottom ends;

a wooden dowel with eyelet screws poked through and screwed into the ceiling or beam and with cup hooks screwed into the dowel;

a wooden poultry crate or wicker bird cage suspended on rope from the ceiling, which could hold lots of utensils or produce;

a discarded basketball hoop attached with screws to the wall or ceiling;

an old wagon wheel fitted out with some "blacksmithy-looking" hooks.

An old metal lampshade frame, provided it is one of the several-

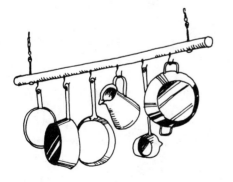 

ribbed, bell-shaped ones, can be the basis of a pot hanger that pins up on the wall. Here's how:

How to Make a Pot Hanger From a Lampshade Frame

Materials and Tools Needed:
one 6-rib, bell-shape lampshade, about 10 inches in length and 9 inches
    in top diameter
wire cutters
heavy-duty pliers
six or seven S-hooks (steel curtain hooks will do)
soldering iron and solder

Directions:
1. Remove all fabric or parchment from the lampshade, until you have bared the frame entirely.
2. With wire cutters, disengage one of the crosspieces at the top of the shade from the top circle.
3. With pliers, bend this crosspiece up at right angles to the other crosspieces and then bend it into a hook.
4. With wire cutters, remove half the top circle of metal, the corresponding half of the bottom circle, and the two ribs on that side of the shade. Now you have a semicircular pot hanger with a hook at the top with which to hang it on the wall.
5. Solder the S-hooks to the bottom edge of the pot hanger at equal

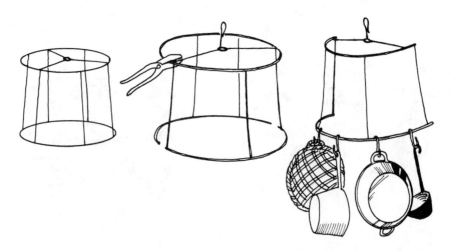

intervals. This soldering isn't absolutely essential if you can achieve a secure mooring of the hooks by mechanical means. Try squeezing them together. If it works, fine; if not, solder, or else a hook will come off the hanger every time you take down a pot.

The second principle I discovered was never to give houseroom to pieces of equipment that weren't multipurpose, thus keeping one's working tools to a minimum. That sounds very easy when your budget is a shoestring one; but you'd be surprised how many middle- or lower-income families consider an electric popcorn-maker *and* an electric frying pan a *must*. Don't go out and buy a semisoft-cheese grater and a deep-fat fryer before you've checked with your M.D. about French-fried foods and your cookbooks about the wisdom of grating semisoft cheese. Resist an ungainly vegetable steamer. When you want to steam vegetables, do it in a strainer suspended over boiling water in a large, covered cooking pot. If you're into canning, *do* get a canning kettle large enough to accommodate more than three jars of preserves; but then, when canning time is over, store nests of ever-diminishing pots and bowls in the kettle, which you can also use for tinting and dyeing without fear of poisoning yourself or your family. The good-looking bean pot you picked up at that flea market last week will be a good decorative holder for your cooking spoons, ladles, spatulas, etc. when you're not baking beans in it.

Before you purchase even one piece of kitchen equipment, see if you can think up *several* uses for it. Then, if it's too large or too expensive anyway, think of how you can use what you already have for the processes you have in mind—and do without it. I've continued to resist the by now nearly ubiquitous electric crockpot; with the heat turned way down as low as possible, my heavy Dutch oven (a wonderful stove-to-table item that was a gift) produces the same results and saves wattage.

Pantries have sort of gone out of style, but there is too little space in most kitchens for the storage of staples and comestibles. On-the-counter containers provide storage and clever kitchen decoration at the same time. Coffee cans with plastic snap-on tops make fine cost-free canisters; they take paint well, too, or can be decorated with adhesive-backed paper. Shaker pantry boxes in round or oval shapes are handsome, as are wooden firkins from some mail-order store such as L. L. Bean in Freeport, Maine, though both these items are devilishly expensive if bought new. Try for a set bought secondhand or collect a set of cake or cookie tins and paint or paper them. An old mailbox painted in one of your kitchen accent colors makes a good bread box.

Herbs and spices are good kitchen decoration, too. Save all those nice little jars that vitamins and pills and capsules are sold in and put your herbs and spices in them. If you recognize all herbs and spices by look and/or smell, you don't have to busy up their appearances with labels; if not, grease-crayon their identity on the tops. Then you might want to make a decorative spice rack to keep them in. Here's an easy one to make.

How to Make a Spice Rack Without the Use of a Drill

Materials and Tools Needed:
two 3/4-inch boards, each 3 × 14 inches (softwood is okay for this)
two 3/4-inch boards, each 3 × 10 inches
four 10-inch lengths of wooden dowel, each 1/2 inch in diameter
twelve flat-headed nails, at least 1 1/2 inches long
hammer
woodworker's glue
wood stain
optional: two small eyelet screws and picture-hanging wire

Directions:
1. With a pencil, mark a spot 3/8 inch from both sides of the corner of one of the longer boards. This is where your first nail will go in. Now mark a spot 3/8 inch from the corner nearest the first corner; then mark a third mark halfway between the first two, on a line with them.
2. On the same side of the board, measure up 7 inches from the first line of marks and make three more, aligned with the first three.
3. Repeat steps 1 and 2 on the second 14-inch board. These are the sides of the spice rack.
4. The shorter boards are, of course, the shelves. Take one 10-inch board and line its end up at a right angle with one of the 14-inch boards. Using the first marks you made to guide you, hammer

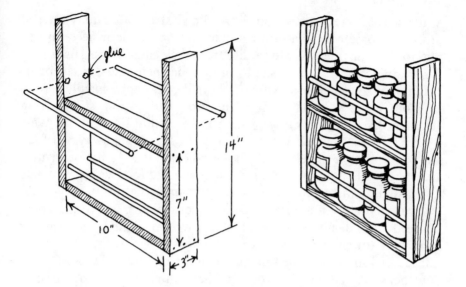

three nails through the outside of the 14-inch board and into the end of the 10-inch board.

5. With the second set of marks, repeat this procedure, attaching the top shelf of the rack to one side.
6. Now it is a simple matter to line the second side up with the ends of the two shelves. Hammer the second half dozen nails in.
7. With a pencil mark the spots where you want the ends of the dowels to go, probably about 2 1/4 inches up from the top of each shelf and 3/8 inch in from the front and back edge of the sides.
8. Mix up your glue and apply it liberally to each end of the four dowels. Then just slide the dowels into place, centering their ends on the marks you made in step 7.
9. Wipe off excess glue and let it dry overnight.
10. Apply wood stain.

You now have a standing spice rack that can be placed anywhere in the kitchen. If you wish to hang it on the wall, simply use the optional picture-hanging screws and wire and pretend you are hanging a picture. In this case you can do with only two dowels, omitting those on the back of the shelves.

Some kind of hardwood cutting surface is necessary in every cooking and food-preparing room. If you lack one, hang around while a road crew works on a tree-lined street after an electrical storm or some other natural disaster that has made it necessary to cut down some trees. Ask for a slice from their chain saws. That's how I got my decorative and useful—in fact indispensable—kitchen cutting board. A decorator I know, believe it or not, obtained hers (one of stout hickory wood, with all its growth rings and still bearing its rugged, nubby bark) by picking it up off the sidewalk on West 11th Street in New York City. Just don't let the highwaymen foist on you a section of felled telephone pole. It's dandy for other uses (see page 61), but can't be used for preparing foods, since it tends to be soaked with creosote or some such untasty substance.

Even if you're an automatic dishwasher devotee, you're still going to need a few dish towels. Don't let any well-meaning friends shower you with towels with complicated designs. Pictorializations of the Statue of Liberty stamped in garish colors or embroideries of fighting cocks may be their idea of just what you need, but hanging them around your kitchen will stamp you as "low rent." Give those towels to the local charity thrift shop or use them for the insides of hot-pot holders (see page 208). Pick out cotton toweling in the local dry goods store that goes with your kitchen color scheme without making a big, elaborate point of it. A yard and a quarter of 27-inch toweling, cut across its width into four equal parts, the edges simply hemmed up by hand or machine, will give you four dish towels, 19 by 25 inches. Cost: approximately 75 cents. Hanging in an airy, drying-out spot, such inexpensive towels can contribute to your decoration far better than the fussy, dust-catching curtains so often found in kitchens. When you take down the ruffles and flounces you might want to turn *them* into dish or fingertip towels.

If you cook in a room with very high ceilings (like those in Federal-style houses or turn-of-the-century apartments), you may feel that all those high-up shelves are just so much wasted space, as indeed they would be if there weren't so many occasional items in most kitchens or pantries. Paint inside of the shelves a dark color. (Hot air rises, carrying with it dust, grease, and sometimes even food particles.) Store things like your collection of less-often-consulted cookbooks, pickling spices and tools, cut-flower vases, and the wok that a misguided friend bought you for a house gift on these shelves.

Incidentally, if you *are* into Chinese cooking, but can't get the hang of using the wok on your flat electric or gas burner, you're right; it doesn't really work. You're better off stir-frying in a plain, large flat-bottomed skillet. Also, there is such a thing as a wok ring, but it costs far more than it should in stores. Fashion one yourself by picking up a flat piece of metal, about 2 inches wide, and bending it into a hoop. Or get one of those metal casserole holders. They're easy to find at local thrift shops because people can't figure out what to do with them once the glass dishes that fit inside are broken. I saw a great one in a Connecticut Good Will shop for 25 cents.

But I digress. High shelving (which we had just painted) gives you an excuse to equip your kitchen with one of those clever step-stool-seats, in which the steps fold under the sitting surface. If you don't find one in the secondhand shop, go to an unpainted furniture store, get a tall wooden round-seat stool, and paint it your favorite kitchen color. Or go to a garbage dump or a hardware store for a nail keg. Kegs make excellent kitchen stools, either in the natural wood (sand it down in the interests of skin or nylon hosiery) or painted to harmonize with your kitchen color scheme. A round foam-rubber top, covered with the same cotton as your dish towels, dresses it up a bit besides cushioning the seat of your pants.

An old metal milk can works in the same way. Beg one from behind the barn of the local dairy farm; there you might get it free or for 2 dollars, whereas in an antique shop you could pay up to 200 dollars for it. Either of these objects looks somehow less "cute" in a skullery than when used as an umbrella stand or end table in the parlor or front entranceway.

The plain wooden stepstool—a utilitarian object that you may

think adds little or nothing to your kitchen decoration and is too low to be used as a seat—makes a very good plant stand when it's not being stepped upon. Don't chop it up for firewood.

Buying stoves, refrigerators, even kitchen sinks secondhand represents such a saving that I wonder why everyone doesn't do it when decorating his or her cooking room. You may be fearful of getting a lemon; but that can happen with brand-new equipment, too, straight from the warehouse and installed at a far greater cost. Read the local newspaper's classified sections, shop around, and then get a guarantee in writing, signed by the seller, that he'll repair it if it breaks down within a year. (It's hard to build in obsolescence that will take place in 367 days exactly.) I happen to feel very strongly about double stainless steel sinks, but porcelain is almost as easy to keep clean, and I'd accept one of those marvelous old stone sinks in a trice if it were to be embedded in a large, sunny, airy, eat-in country kitchen!

If your kitchen is eat-in, but neither country nor large, I know of a dinette set (that's what is *used* to be called) that you, yes even you, can make in a few hours—two benches and a table that will fit into a small kitchen and any period or style of decoration. For this project it would be good to have a drill, though I suppose you *could* make screw holes by pounding nails through first.

How to Make a Kitchen Bench From Five Pieces of Wood

Materials and Tools Needed:
one 3/4-inch hardwood board, 11 1/4 × 22 inches, with corners
   rounded off (for the seat)
two 3/4-inch boards, each 10 1/4 × 16 7/8 inches, with ends cut at a
   35 degree angle (for the legs)
two 1/2-inch boards, trapezoidal in form, each with ends 8 1/2 inches
   and the sides 14 inches and 17 3/4 inches (for the braces)
drill and drill bit
twelve round-head screws, at least 1 inch in length
woodworker's glue

Directions:
   1. With a pencil mark a spot at one corner of one brace board, 3/4
      inch from the side and 1/2 inch from the end; this is where your
      first screw hole will be drilled.

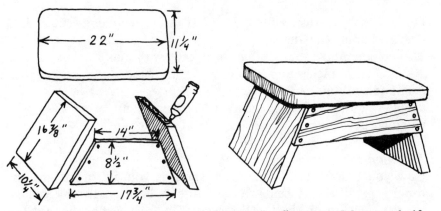

2. Repeat step 1 at the corner nearest the first one. Measure half-way between these first two marks on a line with them and mark the third screw hole.
3. Repeat steps 1 and 2 on the other end of the same side of the brace board.
4. Repeat steps 1, 2, and 3 on the second brace board.
5. Drill holes completely through these twelve locations.
6. Align one marked end of one brace board with the edge of the side of one of the leg boards, and, with a thin pencil, mark the leg board through the screw holes in the brace board.
7. Now drill screw holes to a depth of 3/4 inch in the leg board, using these three marks to guide you.
8. Repeat steps 6 and 7 at the other end of the brace board.
9. Repeat steps 6, 7, and 8 on the other side of the two leg boards.
10. Assemble the base of the bench by screwing screws through these twelve holes.
11. Mix up glue and apply it liberally to the rectangle that forms the top of the bench base.
12. Set the seat board on the base, centering it. Place weights on the bench and let it dry overnight.
13. Stain, paint, or wax the bench to finish it according to your taste and kitchen color scheme.

How to Make the Table to Go With the Benches

Materials and Tools Needed:
one 3/4-inch hardwood board, 15 × 30 inches, with corners rounded
   off (for the tabletop)

two 3/4-inch boards, each 10 1/4 × 31 inches, with ends cut at a 35
  degree angle (for the legs)
1/2-inch boards, trapezoidal in form, each with ends 8 1/2 inches and
  the sides 20 inches and 25 inches (for the braces)
drill and drill bit
twelve round-head screws, at least 1 inch in length
woodworker's glue

Directions:

Now you follow exactly the same steps as you did in making the
bench, the difference being that it will be a bit more trouble centering the tabletop on the finished base. The long side of the tabletop
won't be flush with the edges of the top of the table base, as was the
case with the bench.

1. With a pencil and a ruler, draw lines on the underside of the tabletop that bisect the area first by length and then by width. Where
   these two lines cross is the exact center of the board.
2. Measure the length and width of the top of the finished base.
3. Starting from the center cross on the underside of the tabletop,
   measure half the width of the table base along the width axis in
   one direction and make a mark. Then do the same in the opposite
   direction and make another mark.
4. Starting again from the center cross, measure half the length of
   the table base along the length axis in one direction and make a
   mark. Then do the same in the opposite direction and make another mark.
5. Using these four new marks as guides, draw a pencil rectangle on
   the underside of the tabletop.
6. When the glue is ready on the top of the base, just match up the
   rectangle drawn on the underside of the tabletop with the top of
   the table base. Don't forget to weight the new table while the glue
   dries.
7. Finish the table in the same manner as you did the bench or
   benches.

   This dinette set will take up very little room in your miniscule
kitchen, because, when not being sat upon, the benches will slide
underneath the table, one on each side. When two people are eating
at the table, both sets of feet will fit underneath.

   Since most kitchens these days, whether city, country, or small-

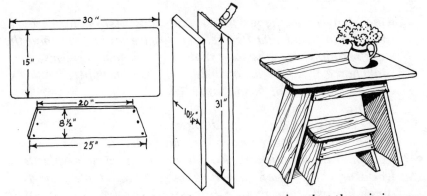

town, are not of the eat-in variety, I am assuming that there is in your house a room especially for dining, usually called a "dining room." If, however, one region of your BIG kitchen, the foyer of your apartment, or the short end of your L-shaped living room is where you habitually eat, then you may still go ahead and read the next chapter: nearly everything in it applies equally to "the dining area." Just, please, don't call it that. The place where such delightful events as the nourishment of yourself and your family or the entertainment of your friends and guests go on deserves a better name than "the dining area." It sounds so cold, inhuman, soul-less, and, well, architectural.

Tips

- *Borrow a trick from a clever workshop-organizer for the kitchen. Nail a row of screw-top jar lids to the underside of an up-high wooden cabinet or shelf. Fill the jars that fit the lids with "display" foodstuffs: flours and grains, various colors and textures of sugar, interestingly shaped pasta. (Simply screw the jars into the nailed-up lids when you're not using them in cooking.)*
- *When laying kitchen floor covering that is flexible, run it up the toe space to the jutting-out bottom of cabinets and other installations. This will facilitate kitchen-floor-washing considerably.*
- *On your trips to a really good town dump wear sturdy gloves and boots. You may want to wade around and turn things over. I've almost never gone to my dump and come away empty-handed, though I must admit that on my most recent foray the pickings*

were slim. In exchange for several pails of organic garbage, some scrap wood that had refused to give up its nails, and the week's supply of asbestos-exhaling, book-mailing bags, all I took home was a scrap of lined composition paper, blank except for these words at the top:

   Scott,

      I can't quite get my head together . . .

A poor bargain, it seemed to me, but better luck next time.

• *If you plan to do much work with attaching fabric or plastic to wood or composition, a very good aid is a staple gun. They range in cost from about 5 to nearly 20 dollars, so you might want simply to rent one for a week or so before making the investment.*

2

Eating Room

Architects and interior designers tell us to be certain when shopping for a house or apartment that every room in the place can be entered without going through any other. This stricture obviates most city apartments of less than twelve rooms, as well as a whole range of well-designed houses of yesteryear. The only room sometimes exempted from this ruling is the one in which you eat, the theory being, I guess, that we don't need privacy at meal time, which occurs at regular intervals, and that in between meals the room can be used for any number of other purposes, including the routing of traffic.

Through the dining room of my childhood one pirouetted to get to the sun porch in one direction, the pantry and then kitchen in another, and the front hall and, subsequently, the living room in a third. The dining room also held in one corner the telephone table and stool. (In those dear old days a wall phone or princess-style instrument was not part of the decor of every room; one *sat down* to make a call, daffodil-shaped part in one hand, ear receiver in the other.) In another corner sat my mother's rug-hooking frame and materials, which were in themselves a splendid decorative element. The dining room was a large, square, multifunctional space. I've never owned one such since; more often, I've lived in homes that lack a room specifically for meals. If you have one, count your blessings; and make the room count decoratively.

I can't begin to count the number of "decorator" dining rooms I've seen pictured in classy home decorating magazines that feature pop art on the walls and furry rugs on the floor. I suppose there *are* people who are turned on by staring into a blowup of Marilyn Monroe's bridgework or a Campbell's soup can while they guzzle their vichyssoise. But I'm darned sure that the interior designer who specifies a high-nap rug on the floor under and around the table where people eat meals has never lifted his or her hand to a house-cleaning chore in his or her life! Now shaggy rugs are dandy in some situations; but, unless manning (more likely womanning) the vacuum cleaner for hours on end of drudgery is your idea of a fun way to spend the weekend, don't put a shaggy rug in the eatery, where it will catch each and every cracker crumb or morsel of ground sirloin and hold onto it for dear life. Chairs are almost impossible to move on a hirsute rug, too. So, whatever you do about floor coverings in the dining room at large, see that the flooring under and around the table is of an easy-to-clean nature and that chairs can be slid back and forth with ease.

My own preference is for a bare wood floor in the eating area; parquet is good (and any dummy or weakling can now lay his own, as it comes in adhesive-backed small squares) or any other arrangement of hardwood that is not waxed or polished *too* slippery. If a hardwood floor is not in your picture, try for a very low-nap, closely woven, broadloom carpeting or an area rug with a small-figured overall design. Insist on fast colors that won't bleed when you shampoo the rug with soap and water. See that it is anchored to the floor by some sure means. Slipping on an unfastened-down rug is a risk in any room; but the hazard is multiplied in the dining room, where carrying pots full of hot food may complicate an accident.

Without doubt, the principal piece of furniture in this room is the dining table. Just as obviously, its size is dictated by the number of people who ordinarily eat there and limited by the dimensions of the. room. If two is your family size, and two-by-four (or very little more) your room's measurements—and you delight in entertaining at dinner for eight at eight, why not keep a small, round pedestal-based table in the eatery and a large folding tabletop of plywood in the closet for "occasions"? Or whip out the folding card table for company-dinner-at-two-tables? The tables don't have to "match," nor do they have to be lined up conference-room style.

Remember, too, that your guests will enjoy your hospitality whether or not your chairs are octuplets. Few situations in decoration are quite as boring as a dining room set in which eight look-alike chairs "go with" the table. Besides, it's expensive: groups of chairs in odd numbers are easy to come by for very little money; even secondhand, even for free from dumps or trash pickup stations. People seem to expect things like chairs to come in even-numbered congeries, though dinner parties or families are very often odd numbered. Why is that? A liqueur bottle plus five glasses is "incomplete," hence, cheaper. Likewise, three dining room chairs, whether Queen Anne cherrywood reproductions or Parsons stackable plastic, constitute a broken set, to be picked up for peanuts. I recently came into three iron-framed, black Naugahyde Eames chairs because their owner was somehow embarrassed by them, as if they were committing an unforgivable offense by not being four. She *gave* them to me (knowing me to be a scavenger), together with a round, glossy, black-topped table, which swells to oval with the addition of a slide-in leaf. These four objects occupy my new dining room, dead center, and live happily with the three side, nondescript, nonmatching, blonde wood chairs already there. Orphans of the storm, these last three chairs have interesting enough histories to relate. One was picked up on Lexington Avenue in New York City, where it awaited the garbage pickup of a Friday morning, years ago. Another was once an office chair; bringing it home and covering the orange plastic seat and back

with a discarded green curtain gave it a new identity. The third is a survivor from my first Manhattan apartment, to which it was brought home from a junk shop on Columbus Avenue, thirty years ago. It was to go with a kneehole desk; I think I remember that it cost 4 dollars—nearly everything bought for that arpartment did.

Bentwood side chairs go very well with ladder-back reproductions; ice cream parlor chairs live happily around a dining table with Windsor fan-backs; fiddle-backs or Queen Anne styles marry backless benches without incident; and a melange of all of these types of seating do not really cause eyebrows to raise. Speaking of benches, meeting-house benches can be bought quite reasonably in knockdown reproductions. If your dining table is a longish one, a meeting-house bench along one side works fine. So does an old church pew, which with a good deal of luck and clever timing you can find in a country (or city) auction or secondhand shop. If you stumble on one for a civilized price, grab it. Should it be too long for your purposes or too long to transport, it's a simple matter to cut a section out of the middle and reassemble it. Find a handyman with a chain saw and ask him to saw it into three equal sections. You may even want to make a sofa out of one of the thirds, rather than use it for dining room seating. (See Chapter 6.)

If your dining table is a long rectangular one with a topless bench on each long side (like the redwood picnic suites that can move into the house in winter and serve perfectly well while you're deciding what to do about a more formal table), comfort can be enhanced by the addition of long cushions to the benches. Just cut some foam rubber to the proper size and cover it with a remnant of fabric. Keep the cushions from sliding off the benches by fastening them each with two belts, passed around cushion and wooden bench top and buckled underneath.

That formal dining table just mentioned need not set you back six months' salary. Decide on what dimensions your room can accommodate and make a dining table in one of the following ways:

Order a flush door from a "door store" or lumber company and glue it to the tops of two ceramic birdbath pedestals. These items are always getting thrown out by people who have carelessly allowed their tops to be smashed.

Buy a length of 3/4-inch plywood; cover it with felt stretched tight across its surface and nailed to the edges of the plywood with decorative upholstery nails. Screw into the underside of the plywood four iron legs bought in the five-and-ten, hardware store, or office furniture shop.

See the project that follows.

How to Make a Dining Table Out of Paneling

Materials and Tools Needed:
five 5-foot lengths of 5-inch tongue-and-groove paneling
two 3/4-inch boards, each 6 × 26 inches
twenty screws, at least 1 inch long
drill and drill bit
woodworker's glue
four lengths of 2 × 4s, each about 2 1/2 feet long (This kind of paneling can often be found where a barn or silo is falling into disrepair. If you're not that lucky, plain straight-edged boards will do.)

Directions:
1. Line the paneling up tongue-to-groove, or the straight-edge boards edge-to-edge.
2. Apply woodworker's glue to the edges (except the two outer ones) and push them together.
3. Put the tabletop flat on the floor, and, with a sturdy piece of furniture, wedge one edge firmly against the wall. Leave it in this position overnight.
4. Measure 1 inch in from both sides of one corner of one 3/4-inch board and mark your first screw hole.
5. Repeat step 4 on the corner nearest the first one.
6. Repeat steps 4 and 5 at the other end of the same side of the board.
7. Aligned with these first four marks, make six more marks that will fall roughly in the center of the three interior tabletop boards when the board you're marking is stretched across the tabletop at right angle.
8. Repeat steps 4, 5, 6, and 7 on the second 3/4-inch board.
9. Drill holes completely through these twenty locations.
10. Place the two brace boards 6 inches from either end of the tabletop, on its underside. With a thin pencil, mark drill spots on the underside of the tabletop through the drilled holes in the brace boards.

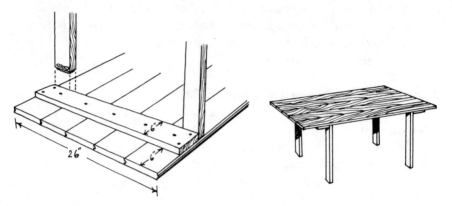

11. Drill holes in these new marked sites to a depth of 1/4 inch.
12. Screw the brace boards to the tabletop.
13. Apply glue to one end of each 2-by-4; apply glue 3/4 inch down the 4-inch side as well.
14. With the tabletop still upside down on the floor, attach the glued ends of the four legs to the right angle formed by the edge of the brace board and the underside of the tabletop, one at each corner.
15. Leave table in this position for half the drying time of the glue.
16. Turn the table right side up and allow the glue to finish drying with the weight of the top against the tops of the legs.

   Voilà! A banquet table fit for nobility!

   If your dining room is spacious enough to accommodate a table large enough for company plus the dinner-party number of seats (matching or not), you doubtless have no traffic problems and can leave the chairs while not in use scattered around the room here and there. But may I put in a word for *not* lining them up against walls? There's something reminiscent of dancing school about that method of furniture arrangement. Besides, if you leave the chairs *at* the table, even when only one or two are dining, you can do fun things with the walls. Like, for instance:

   Buy molding by the foot and use it for a plate rail. Wallpaper below it, paint above it, and exhibit your collection of sea-shells or Dresden figurines on the plate rail, or your few choice pieces of Wedgwood or pewter.

   Get your art-student relative to practice on the walls by paint-ing an over-all mural, perhaps an outdoor scene to make the room look larger.

Get yourself a stained-glass kit and put together a mosaic "window" on the wall.
Frame a handsome scarf of silk paisley or cotton batik on the
   wall or simply stretch it on the wall and fasten with pushpins.
Folding chairs stowed away in a closet and brought out for company are a way to keep the smallish dining room uncluttered, of
course. But don't fall into the trap of stackable metal or plastic chairs.
That is, don't leave them stacked in the corner when you're eating
alone or à deux. Your dining room will look like the church social
hall or like a bistro on "closed" night, unless you hide them behind
a nifty screen. A folding screen doesn't have to be a coromandel or
a relic from the Tang Dynasty. For some easy kinds of screens to
make see Chapter 6.
   In most eating rooms of more than nook proportions, another
piece of furniture is needed: some surface from which to serve food.
It was once true that a buffet was de rigueur, but now, any piece will
do if it has an ample surface for holding your hot tray and other
dishes from which you'll serve or ask guests to serve themselves. As
mentioned in the Introduction, what performs this function in *my*
house is a big, old Victorian mahogany bureau that has seen far better
days. The large drawers serve as a linen closet; table settings (stainless steel flatware) are in the shallower top drawer; and the top is a
serving table. In the house of a male friend the space-at-a-premium
problem is solved by a piece of plywood, 5 by 2 feet, set up on two sawhorses for large dinner parties, which are always buffet style. On other
days the plywood slab and sawhorses go back to the barn, leaving
the small dining room with only a tiny rectangular table and two
(nonmatching, as it happens) chairs.
   If you have in your attic an old Duncan Phyfe secretary, long since
replaced by a businesslike flat-top desk in the study, why not bring
it down to the dining room? Store dishes in the top, linens in the
drawers, and put the desk flap down for a serving surface.
   One of the good things about the dining room (like the kitchen and
bathroom, indeed like the bedroom and living room too) is that it is
so efficaciously decorated with things used in that room. Not the
Spode or Majolica plates you rested on the plate rail, but your every-
day eating ware, when it's not being eaten from, getting renewed
in the dishwasher, or sitting on open or glassed-in shelves. China or
glass, ceramic or porcelain, or even plastic dishes, tumblers, cups,

saucers, and bowls on the shelf can be a handsome, embellishing element, eye-catching as well as handy.

When I was a child there were many complete sets of dinnerware in the dining room; at least four that I can remember. One was an inherited set of fancy Limoges gold-on-white, paper-thin china for twelve; one set of Wedgwood blue-on-white also for twelve; a set of deep-blue willow-pattern ware; and a set of six (the size of our family) vari-colored Fiestaware. The first two were used on holidays and other festive occasions; the second two were our run-of-the-mill lunch and dinner dishes. Breakfast, as I recall it, was eaten from the breakfast dishes (I seem to remember a lot of deep red glass cups and bowls), which were lodged in the kitchen or pantry. That accoutrement required an awful lot of dish-storage space, which fortunately was no problem, what with glass china cabinets, buffets, serving tables, and whatnot in the large-size dining room, not to mention miles of shelves in the pantry. But it wouldn't really go with today's highly mobile life-style. Both the Limoges (no longer complete settings for a dozen diners) and isolated pieces of the Fiestaware have made it, by the way, through many vicissitudes to my own present home—a long and arduous journey. I would just as soon the former hadn't. It's so delicate that I don't dare use it. But, oh, if only the latter had made it; complete Fiestaware is now bringing fancy prices in flea markets and tag sales. It's sort of a first cousin to Depression Glass.

If, because of so many doors and windows, your dining room (like mine) lacks the right space for a china cabinet and you (like me) have not yet arrived at that halcyon state of one-good-set-for-every-day-including-company-dinner-party-days, your extra "good" set of china doubtless stays packed away much of the time. I have a suggestion: let your temporary "china cabinet" be a matched set of wooden bushel baskets that you've picked up. You won't get them from the discards of farmers and other country neighbors who know better, but, gradually, over a period of six months or so, get them one-by-one off the sidewalks near city grocers, who, apparently, don't know what treasures they are throwing out. Fitted out with covers that are scraps of fabric related to something else in the room, they will make a very attractive addition to the dining room decor. These baskets can hold a powerful lot of Limoges; and they fit nicely under windows.

Dining room windows with restful scenes beyond them are a con-comitant to pleasant dining and good digestion. Under-draping them is advisable: perhaps just some neutral batiste or marquisette or woven "glass" curtains falling to the floor at either side of the window. But if what's outside needs blotting out for a quiet dinner hour, perhaps this is the room that gets the cafe curtain treatment. Hang two round rods at top and mid-window and use clip-on curtain rings (which can be bought for something like 10 cents apiece) to save yourself a sewing chore. For the curtains choose a substantial fabric in a color and/or pattern that won't soon suffer from being whisked back and forth by hand. I am partial to dining rooms with soft green walls and rust or tangerine curtains at the windows; but if this complementary-colors scheme doesn't go well with your dinnerware, choose one that will.

The penny-pinching do-it-yourself decorator of today is well advised to think long and hard about dishes. She should opt for *one* set of something classic, simple, and utilitarian that is also available in "open stock," for replacements, even if she is using her dinner plates as "decoration" on an open shelf. For dinnerware that is going to be eaten from plain white or off-white with no stamped-on or baked-in design is best. I think so, anyway, partly because I take special pleasure in the colors and shapes of food and think a stark background shows them off to best advantage. Plain black china is striking, too, and with many meals, such as pasta or rice-based dishes, does very well in designing a good-looking meal. Avocado or delft blue dishes under your luncheon fare just may not blend with the shrimp or steak or baked beans as well. Better to save your flower, animal, or scenic designs in ceramic for the occasional pieces or your cow-shaped pitchers and rooster-form gravy boats for once-in-a-while meals.

Besides allowing your foodstuffs to carry the day designwise, a single all-white set of dishes allows you to effect a color scheme in your choice of table linens and centerpieces. Even if your dining table is a comely oak or walnut surface that you keep in good form by frequently washing and waxing, there are times when you want to dress up with a beautiful linen tablecloth in a seasonal color—plain, of course, trusting the rest of the table setting to provide the textural and design interest. Buy it by the length in a dry goods department and hem it up at home; it won't cost as much that way.

Here are some other notions for tablecloths:
bed sheets or pillowcases stitched together;
couch covers or blanket covers;

drapes that no longer fit your windows;
old evening skirts or maxi-coats;
remnants of dressmaking or upholstery fabric;
a patchwork quilt that has lost its stuffing.

These items are usually fine for square, rectangular, or even oval tables. But, if you have a round table and lust after a big, full, round tablecloth that falls to the floor in soft, opulent folds and all you have is a rectangular piece of cotton, you can probably get a large, round tablecloth out of it by careful cutting. The secret is to cut a semicircular piece out of the middle of the swatch and two pie-shaped pieces on either end of the swatch. First stitch the two pie-shapes together into a semicircle and then stitch the two semicircles together.

There's something very gracious and attractive about a dining table all set for dinner—the crystal goblets sparkling in the candlelight, the tablecloth falling to the floor in graceful folds. This charming picture contains at least three traps, however, for the budget home-entertainer to avoid. In the first place, that falling-to-the-floor damask cloth may do just that. When a diner pulls his chair up to the table or away from it, the cloth may catch in his clothing, foot, or chair leg and bring your dinner party down with a crash, literally. (Don't sneer. I've seen it happen.) Better to stick with a shorter tablecloth for actual dining and leave the to-the-floor covering for between-meal decoration. And see that the cloth is firmly anchored to the table, possibly by an underpinning of felt, rubber, or rubberlike plastic that will also provide insulation for your tabletop. If it's a dinner after cocktails, possibly the crystal tumblers could be supplanted by glass from the dime store, where you can find sturdy and good, well-designed tumblers these days for about 29 cents apiece, or even plastic for obvious reasons. The candles, even though their flattering light is legendary and they can save you some kilowatts in your electric bill, should also be reserved for occasions when you know you will be having very sober diners. An overly expansive gesture at table can result in a bonfire and maybe even an expensive lawsuit. (Yes, I've known this to happen too.) The least it can do is wreck your centerpiece.

The centerpiece is one very efficient way of keeping your decoration dynamic and lively. Change it often. While I can't think of anything more delightful than a bowl of fresh flowers if it's midsummer and you live in the country or adjacent to a blooming penthouse, flowers are not the only way to decorate your dining table for peanuts. Consider, as well, the following:

a piece of wood or ceramic sculpture;
a beautiful covered soup tureen;
a single branch of apple blossoms;
a platter of fallen leaves in autumn colors;
a bowl of fresh green Swiss chard leaves;
the animal your child made out of modeling clay that day;
a vase full of fresh field flowers and stalks of basil;
a good-looking basket with some philodendra in it;
a cutting board with a loaf of freshly baked bread on it.

The last centerpiece item I'll mention is my favorite and it's for my less formal entertaining. Edible centerpieces often do double duty, too, by providing the dessert. Even if your dinner is going to end with cheese and crackers, why not arrange a platter or bowl of fresh whole fruits in advance and let it be the table's centerpiece? There's nothing like the contemplation of a handsomely arranged cornucopia of nuts and fruit to discourage your guests from over-eating the entrée.

Floral centerpieces don't have to be roses from a posh florist, nor do flowers have to be centerpieces. Shot glasses containing tiny bouquets of herbs or small flowers, one between every two place settings, can enhance dining pleasure. Empty rifle shell cases can also function as miniscule vases. In fact, this is the best use I can think of for those unhappy remnants I frequently find in the woods near my house. Be sure to steady them with a bit of child's modeling clay or window-edging putty wrapped around their bases.

Centerpieces appropriate to the season aren't too corny if you avoid the traditional plastic Santa Claus and reindeer on cotton batting. At Yuletide, why not trim your table instead with a simple branch of pine or fir picked up beside the road or liberated from under the city vendor's ranks of Christmas trees? In autumn a small pumpkin on a sprinkling of autumn leaves is understated and cheerful; and you can cook and eat the pumpkin later. At Passover or Easter time a basket of eggs, tinted or not, organic or marble, are appropriate, and a bit later in the season a single branch of apple blossoms, or, later still, the same branch bearing one perfect crab apple. What could be nicer?

For brunch or luncheon entertaining or anything less formal than evening dinner, the bare wood of a well-cared-for table is splendid—warm and welcoming. But sometimes you may want to go the place mat way. Place mats don't have to be those horrible laminated plastic objects with Queen Elizabeth or an American flag inside. Think about the following for place mats:

last year's shirt or dress back;

woven straw;

faded upholstery fabric you took off a chair;

leftover squares or pieces of asphalt or linoleum floor covering;

gift dish towels still too full of sizing to work well as dish towels;

discarded nylon hose or panty hose, cut in narrow strips (some lengthwise, some in rounds), and then braided and wound into rounds or ovals. (See page 119 for directions for making a rag rug and apply these principles on a smaller scale.)

Flat silver is almost a thing of the past; at least it is no longer the sine qua non of the bride of today. And why should it be when stainless steel eating utensils, which set you back far less, come in so many handsome patterns? Also, the liberated householder doesn't have all that time to waste keeping silver clean and sparkling. I recommend not buying sterling silver flatware, but I *do* recommend that you bring home all the wooden stirrers, mustard containers, plastic spoons, forks, and knives, and tiny pepper and salt shakers you can preserve from fast food restaurants. They are of inestimable value and are useful in a thousand ways in your kitchen, workroom, bathroom, garden, and so on. They are free, too, whereas at cut-rate stores you can pay up to a dollar for a plastic table setting.

Oil and vinegar cruets, available by the dozens at auctions and junk shops for pennies, if good-looking, should not be hidden away, but left in the dining room for purposes of decoration, as well as handiness. Let your guests "dress" their own salads. If you have a friend who works in a chemistry laboratory, beg a couple of glass lab bottles with glass stoppers from him. These bottles come in several sizes and they have lovely lines.

Just as smart shoppers of a small size head for the children's department when buying shoes and some other articles of clothing, the budget home decorator makes a beeline for the little girl's toy department when searching for some kinds of home accessories. They cost less there. Take a demitasse set, for example. Why not simply buy a child's tea set, which is made up of cups and saucers in demitasse size? When searching for a little chest to put on your bureau for jewelry, hairpins, or the like, or for stamps, paper clips, and rubber bands for your desktop, doesn't it make sense to go and case the dollhouse furniture?

If you're really into saving money on dishes to serve or eat from, don't forget the charming convention of serving food in "natural" containers. Is there anything more beautiful for dessert than a combination of fresh fruits served in a scooped-out watermelon shell? Or using a bell pepper hollowed out to pass the cold condiments in? Celery stalks stuffed with various cheeses can be passed with equanimity at a stand-up cocktail party; and the soup course, whether hot or cold, becomes a conversation stimulator when served in a hollowed-out pumpkin or winter squash.

Shells, naturally, make perfect servers for fish and seafood dishes; but why stop at baking clam mixes in clamshells, snails with butter and garlic in snail shells? Save the shell of the next lobster and use it to serve tuna salad in. Put your chick-pea or avocado appetizer into individual clam or oyster shells. Water and wine can be drunk from some large shells or from gourds for that matter.

If, despite all your protestations, you do inherit a costly and fragile set of drinking goblets, don't throw away the member that soon acquires a crack or chip. The same advice applies, naturally, to your Royal Daulton china cups, bowls, saucers, and plates. Use the slightly cracked glass or damaged cup for:

a flower vase;
a cigarette holder;
a breadstick server;
a carrot or celery stick holder;
a plant pot;
a brush-and-comb container;
a toothbrush holder;
even a do-nothing piece of decor on the top shelf, with chip or
   crack turned to the wall.

Saucers that have lost their mates become:
ashtrays;
plant pot moisture catchers;
coasters;
and all manner of things.

Color is important in dining rooms. Digestion is aided, we hear, by relaxation; thus, you don't want to use gobs of hot, exciting colors like fire-engine red. The neutral shades or those on the "cool" side of the spectrum are more appropriate in the large expanses, such as floors, walls, ceilings, tablecloths. Lighting, which, of course, is a part of color at night (or in an interior, windowless room), should be soft and indirect. If you don't have light in the form of wall brackets, place lamps in corners—either floor lamps or shaded table lamps. Or, bounce a bar of light from a tube lamp off your ceiling and onto the table.

If you have table lamps for your dining room corners, but nothing

to put them on, you can get them to the right height by making pedestals for them. Following is an easy one, which can double as a plant
stand, sculpture holder, and any number of other uses.

How to Make a Lamp Pedestal From Some Tomato Fencing

The kind of rectangular-hole fencing needed here, sometimes called
"tomato gard," can be found in hardware stores, even in cities.

Materials and Tools Needed:
one square of steel fencing, 3 × 3 feet, with wire tabs remaining at
   one side
fabric remnant of the same size
plastic wash basin with curled back lip, 12 1/4 to 12 3/4 inches in
   diameter across the top
pliers
needle and thread

Directions:
1. By rolling the fencing on the floor, bend the fencing into a cylinder if, as is unlikely, it isn't already in one.
2. With pliers twist the wire tabs at one edge of the fencing around
   the other edge to hold the cylindrical form.
3. Wrap the fabric around the cylinder and sew it to the steel wire
   at four points at the top of the cylinder and then four points at
   the bottom of the cylinder.
4. Hand sew the fabric together down the length of the cylinder.
5. Place the basin in the top of the cylinder; its slightly longer diameter, plus the lip, will hold it firmly in place.
6. Position lamp, plant, or whatever squarely in the middle of the
   basin; its weight will anchor the pedestal in place.
   A similar plant or lamp stand can be made by nailing together four
boards, 3/4 by 3 feet, into a rectangular tube and then gluing a square
of wood to the top, or placing a metal or plastic tray on the top.
   If you opted for the steel-and-fabric lamp stand, it would be a good
idea to cover a lampshade with a bit of the same fabric. Again, simply
sew it top and bottom to the lampshade frame and then hem it by
hand where it joins. For more casual lamps to make from detritus,
see Chapter 6.

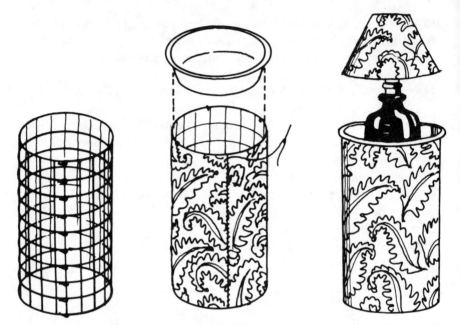

In my mind (and sober household) one of the principal forms of decoration appropriate to dining rooms is candles in candlesticks or candelabra. Even if never lighted, candles are a quick and easy form of dressing up a room. Like most items made or sold originally in pairs, candleholders can be picked up very cheap at tag sales or junk shops when single. Or, you can fashion them yourself from any material with a little give to it. Try making candlesticks in the following ways:

gouge a hole out of a block of cork;

coil some heavy wire into a cylindrical shape that gets wider for the last three or four coils (for the base);

wind some "snakes" of plastic putty inside those unused napkin rings;

look in your workshop collection of nuts and bolts to see if there are any large nuts or other odd pieces of metal that will hold candles;

use a Gibson Gripper glued to a square plastic base.

Candleholders don't have to match. In fact, here's a very clever piece of casual decoration: a row of candles of different values of one color in candlesticks that vary in size and shape. The candlesticks can vary from a tall, floor-standing, etched brass, round job to a

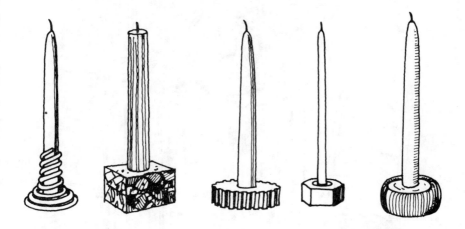

nubby, little, square, ceramic one with a finger handle attached to the side. The candles might march along one wall of the room, the shorter ones on a narrow low wooden platform knocked together out of scrap wood. This is far more amusing than elaborate candelabra hanging from the ceiling. In any case, the important thing about dining room lighting is to keep it soft.

If your lighting is irretrievably bare globe, be sure that the bulbs are the frosted kind. There's nothing that can spoil a dinner plate's come-hither look more easily than glaring, bright light. Try to avoid some kinds of neon tubes, too: mauve mashed potato just isn't appealing, nor is the dead-skin look some kinds of lighting impart to human faces.

Eating rooms, any size, seem to acquire all sorts of decorative elements, depending on who owns them. I knew a columnist-commentator who put a carousel horse in hers. My mother's dining room, it seems to me, besides all the artsy-craftsy equipment, once held my brother's rocking horse, as well as my dollhouse—items which wouldn't have found asylum there if we'd had a proper playroom or enough bedrooms to go around. In countless dining room windows all over the country are massed collections of houseplants. A miniature greenhouse can be installed without much trouble in a dining

room window. The large dining room is an ideal spot for an aquarium, especially if it's a room that the cat can be kept out of. A tank full of tropical fish can be a fascinating design element; landscape it with coral and water plants, and try to avoid miniature statues, sunken treasure chests, and the like. With a soft light behind the aquarium at night, this accessory is a soothing, relaxing concomitant to dinner at nine.

If you do have room in your dining area for a cabinet to hold dishes and such, don't imagine you are limited to a Welsh dresser or an Early American hutch or a standard assemble-it-yourself corner cabinet. If, at an auction, you find a Victorian book case or whatnot shelf, what's to stop you from using that? Should your grandmother finally decide to throw out her old pine icebox, that relic from the prerefrigerator days, talk her out of it and install that near antique in your dining room. The other day in a large department store I saw one "taken down" to the grain of the wood (I assume it had borne several coats of paint) but not otherwise changed in any way. There was a price tag of over 200 dollars on it. If your doctor-husband or dentist-friend is refurbishing his office, see if you can capture one of those lovely old instrument chests with the little flat drawers. They make wonderful cabinets for knives, forks, spoons, and napkins; and one or two of the drawers can be pulled out while plants, clay statues made by your children, or other decorative items are stationed in them.

Just, please, don't turn the old-fashioned coffee grinder into a lamp base; don't put candles into Chianti bottles; and, most of all, DON'T put the furry rug under the dining table. If you're not addicted to crackers in bed, bedside is the place for the fur or loop-wool or flokati rug, or in front of the fireplace. If you have a fireplace in dining room *and* living room, lucky you. See Chapters 3 and 6 for some good fireplace ideas.

Tips

- *Linen napkins in a variety of colors are a pretty part of the table setting for a dinner party. Labor-saving hint: put the napkins in shades of red where you are seating the people who still insist on wearing lipstick.*
- *Convert a tablecloth designed for a rectangular table to one for an oval table by slicing off the corners. Then sew the sliced-off portions together into two matching square napkins, and hand hem the four corners of the tablecloth.*
- *Never scorn trashbin, dump, or incinerator room finds that seem incomplete. There is a high mortality rate among the bottom parts of, for example, glass- or china-covered dishes, leaving dozens of perfectly good covers. Take them home; never pass by whole covers. You may have something the lids will fit, if not now then in the future. That's how I assembled two magnificent large glass apothecary jars—tops from a Connecticut glass-recycling center, jars from a Manhattan sidewalk trash can—and my covered iron skillet. Even if you can't make a perfect marriage, you may be able to use the mateless objects for some*

wall hanging or homegrown collage or even shatter some pottery to put under your plant-potting soil for aeration and drainage.

- Who would have believed during the Great Depression that Depression Glass would in thirty-odd years become collectors' items, or that tin toys would now be bringing prices in the thousands of dollars? Remember that today's junk is tomorrow's antique and stake out some artifact of today that may become a treasure in a generation.
- Remember that all-cotton fabrics should be washed before you start working with them, unless they are marked "preshrunk." Most blends, such as cotton and polyester, don't require preshrinking.
- In constructing furniture out of wood, remember that a triangular gusset (small piece of wood) added to corners makes for added stability.

3

Sleeping Room

This chapter would be called "The Bedroom," except for two things: one, so many people don't enjoy the luxury of a room reserved exclusively for sleeping, and two, countless thousands the world over don't sleep in beds. Among this latter group are Asians and others who stretch out on the floor with or without some sort of mat or padding to save their bones from hard surfaces; people who habitually sleep in sleeping bags in or out of doors; and those who prefer hammocks. (You may be surprised to learn that men who have spent most of their lives at sea are not the only people who enjoy sleeping in hammocks.)

The hammock or Murphy bed sleepers are, for the most part, small-apartment dwellers whose special problems of sleeping room will be taken up in more detail in Chapter 9. This chapter, then, can be devoted to what we used quaintly to call "The Bedroom," a separate room large enough to accommodate a bed and at least one other piece of furniture.

Some years ago, I was shocked to hear a lady, who was examining my bedroom, ask me when I was going to "finish it." I looked around for scuffed floorboards, peeling furniture paint, filthy walls and/or some other condition of unfinish or disrepair in which I could have been remiss—and found none. Then I realized that she was alluding to the fact that my husband and I didn't have a "bedroom suite," without which she felt no bedroom could possibly be considered "finished." Since she was not a decorator looking for a job, but my mother-in-law, I couldn't "pish-tush" her; so I mumbled something or other about temporary quarters and then attributed to the generation gap the fact that she didn't admire our bedroom as much as I did.

Let's see if I can remember this bit of ancient history. The box spring sat right on the floor. (Later, when we could afford the 13 dollars extra, we bought a steel frame on wheels. I notice in the newspapers and television ads today that this device is often "thrown in" for free when you purchase a spring-and-mattress set in some emporia.) The spring, together with the foam-rubber mattress that accompanied it, set us back something like 59 dollars, on sale. It costs slightly more nowadays, of course, but not significantly. That bargain bed performed yeoman service for about twenty years. (After two decades foam rubber begins to disintegrate; and its odor, too, becomes unpleasant.) There was no headboard or footboard either, but a beautiful hand-hooked rug hung on the wall at the bed's head. The spread was narrow-wale corduroy in turkey red and picked up one of the colors in the hooked rug. The fabric was bought in a remnant shop. It was just long and wide enough, cut in half and sewn together, to fall to the floor in an opulent manner. (See page 65 for how to get mileage out of a narrow-width piece of fabric.)

The little bedside tables for holding lamps, clocks, books, etc., didn't match; in fact, they weren't tables at all. One was a little square-seated oak stool that had once been my mother's dining room telephone seat. (The telephone *table* had long since disappeared.) The other bedside table was a nail keg, found on the city sidewalk, painted black. I think my mother-in-law was a little happier when I "dressed" the nail keg in a blue-flowered, cotton-print, dirndl skirt from my wardrobe. Remember dirndls—those jobs we used to dry after laundering by winding them around a broomstick? The only other piece of furniture in the room, which was a small one with more than its share of doors to break up the wall space, was a gargantuan mahogany-veneer chest of drawers, bought for a song in a secondhand shop. An orphan piece left over from what probably had once been a many-splendored bedroom suite, it had a turn-of-the-century look, as if it had once had brother and sister dressing tables, armoires, chests-on-chests, and such. Its shiny surface I removed with turpentine, producing a softer effect. (See Chapter 2 to find out its present employment.)

A full-length mirror, left behind by the previous tenants of the apartment, hung on one of the room's three doors, and a colorful, large poster decorated one wall. The only thing wrong with that room, in my eyes, was that there was no place to put the nice warm-red spread at night. No room at the foot of the bed for the usual stool, bench, or trunk that might hold the spread; no chair to throw it over while we slept. That situation was soon remedied by the acquisition (from my parents' overfurnished house, though it might just as well have been from the sidewalk or the incinerator room) of a luggage rack. It is a most useful accessory, even if you have to buy one, whose great advantage in a tiny bedroom is that it folds up and slips out of sight in a closet or behind a door, curtain, or piece of furniture. (My favorite present-tense luggage rack serves, with the addition of an old birch bread board, as a chair-side lamp table in the living room.)

The folding luggage rack is not the only answer to the bedspread-holding decoration problem, of course. There are a number of solutions that cost little or nothing and use up hardly any space:

a standing towel rack;

a gentleman's dressing frame;

a metal folding eat-in-front-of-the-TV table (often found thrown away on city sidewalks);

a weathered apple-tree branch "planted" in a bucket of sand;

a child's trapeze (perhaps suspended between two windows, its ropes attached to the curtain rods);

a rickety, no-longer-used rug-hooking frame.

In miniscule city-apartment bedrooms with low ceilings, as well as upstairs bedrooms in a Cape Cod or any cottage where the walls slant, you may find that by placing the box spring right on the floor you will achieve exactly the right height when the mattress is added. That is definitely the case in my own present-day bedroom. Before I realized this, I made a bedstead, anyway, which would be a perfect foundation for a bed in a high-ceilinged room. Since it cost me zero dollars—literally nothing, aside from a bit of pleasant labor—I didn't mind taking it apart again and storing the parts in the garage. There had been no cost because I had picked up some two-by-fours from an abandoned house-building site. If you can't do that, try the local dump or junk collection yard; used lumber is often seasoned and so is less subject than new wood to the swelling and shrinking caused by changes in temperature and humidity. I happened to have already possessed the necessary hardware. Last, but not least, come the legs, which were a gift of the State of Connecticut. You know how often along the sides of country roads you see hunks of old (and long since replaced) telephone poles lying around? Keep your eye on one such relic; and the next time the road crew is on hand with its electric saw, cutting off tree limbs for road visibility or to free telephone wires, or whatever, dash out with your yardstick and ask them very politely if they would just saw that old telephone pole remnant into four 10-inch lengths for you. That's how I got *my* bed legs.

How to Make a Bed Frame for a Full-Size Springs-and-Mattress

Materials and Tools Needed:
seven 2 × 4s (actually 1 1/2 × 3 1/2 inches), each 74 3/4 inches long
two 3/4-inch boards, each 7 1/2 inches × 4 feet 6 inches
twenty-eight flat-headed screws at least 2 inches long
drill and drill bit
screwdriver
four 10-inch sections of telephone pole

Directions:
  1. With a ruler and pencil, measure 1 inch in from one end of one of the 3/4-inch boards, 3 inches down from one side, and make a mark. This is your first drill hole.

2. Measure 1 1/2 inches across the board (toward the other side) from the first mark and on a line with it and make your second drill hole mark.
3. At the other end of the same surface of the board, repeat steps 1 and 2.
4. Measure the distance between the two pairs of marks and divide it by six.
5. Using the measurement made in step 4, make five more pairs of marks aligned with the first two pairs this distance apart.
6. Drill holes clear through the 3/4-inch board at all fourteen marks.
7. Repeat steps 1 through 6 with the second 3/4-inch board.
8. Mark corresponding drill holes (on a center line, 1 1/2 inches apart) on both the cut ends of all seven 2-by-4s.
9. Drill holes to a depth of 3/4 inch at all of these twenty-eight marks.
10. Matching up the holes in one board with the holes at one end of the 2-by-4s, screw the 2-by-4s and headboard together.
11. Repeat step 10, using the footboard and the other end of the 2-by-4s.
12. Now your frame is put together and all that remains is to rest it on the four telephone pole sections, one at each corner.

For an extra precaution—or if you anticipate very heavy duty—it would be a good idea to reinforce each of the fourteen right angles with L-shaped metal braces where the undersides of the two-by-fours meet the foot and headboards; this is an optional step.

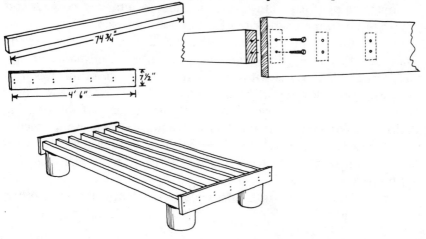

Unpainted-furniture stores sell very inexpensively (50 dollars for the double-bed size in New York City recently) what's called a "storage bed," which is essentially a wooden platform with three large drawers built in. It's even cheaper to construct a sleeping platform yourself. For that you should have a cousin in the plywood business. If he can get it for you wholesale, you've got it made.

How to Build Your Own Sleeping Platform (Double-Bed Size)

Materials and Tools Needed:
one sheet of 5/8-inch plywood, 4 feet 8 inches × 6 feet 4 inches
two 3/4-inch boards, each 5 inches × 6 feet 4 inches
two 3/4-inch boards, each 5 inches × 4 feet 6 1/2 inches
hammer
twelve flat-headed nails, at least 1 1/2 inches in length
woodworker's glue
enough fabric to cover the platform, top, and sides

Directions:
1. Construct the platform frame by hammering nails through the ends of the longer boards into the edges of the shorter boards—three to each corner.
2. Apply glue to the top of the frame just constructed, all around.
3. Lay the plywood slab on top of the frame and line it up squarely.
4. Let the glue harden overnight.
5. Cover the platform with fabric, making hospital-bed corners and stapling it to the inside rim of the support boards.

This platform, which is really just a big lid-less box turned upside down, can be made from scrapwood and an inferior quality of plywood, since it's covered with fabric. If you have beautiful wood to work with (for the support boards), you will want to provide 1-inch wood edging for the plywood and miter its corners. If the sleeping platform becomes a permanent installation, you may want to consider carpeting it to match the floor covering of the room. (Remember that you won't need to carpet the portion of the platform that will be covered by the mattress.)

Now all you have to do is add a mattress—foam rubber or other. If you have access to a foam-rubber manufacturing company or out-

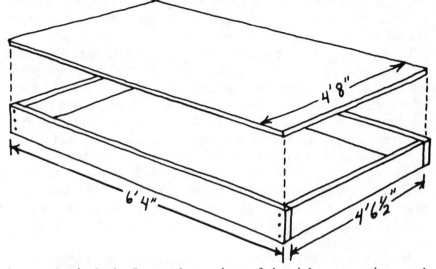

let, you're in luck. Just order a piece of the right proportions and then sew it into a cotton cover or zip it into an already-made one. This will be a lot cheaper than buying a mattress ready-made. Don't imagine, by the way, that 5 inches of foam between you and a straight, hard surface, such as a floor or plywood platform, will be insufficient or uncomfortable. If up to now you've been sleeping on a squishy, lumpy kapok or hair mattress, you won't believe how much better you'll feel after you change to the flat, firm surface.

A Ping-Pong tabletop, begged from a friend about to trade it in for a pool table, serves as sleeping platform in a loft I helped decorate. The tabletop is simply laid on an H-shaped frame of wood. Some converted barns have interesting sleeping rooms, too. One owner has remained true to the ways of his forebears and has left the hay-loft in the barn, reachable by ladder as it always was. The loft is the bedroom, and he achieved this by spreading on the floorboards a couple of mattresses covered in red and blue bandana prints. (This loft arrangement, incidentally, appears in some of the barnlike pre-fabricated houses now on the market.)

I persuaded another barn dweller to leave in place two box stalls, which, with the addition of bunks to one stall and an auction-bought, four-poster bedstead to the other stall, serve very nicely as guest rooms. The master bedroom in this converted barn is in the ex-silo, which has been partitioned off into three levels with an iron spiral staircase connecting. The top level is only half a floor, which is the sleeping platform (a very snug and private one), curtained off from the master bath–dressing-room below it.

Positioning a bed in a small conventional bedroom seems to give some people a lot of trouble. Sometimes there is only one place where a double bed can possibly go—but sometimes not. To complicate matters, there may be both an ideal summer position and the coziest place to sleep in winter. Look more closely, and don't rule out the diagonal (or kitty-corner) approach, which can add drama to the decoration of a room that would otherwise be as trite and dull as dishwater. In a room with windows on every wall, where cross-ventilation would otherwise blow right onto the bed, placing a bed's head across the corner of the room is sometimes the best way to avoid too much exposure to the snows of winter or the rains of the monsoon season.

Unless you're about to weave them yourself, there's very little opportunity for saving money on bed linens. Naturally, you buy them only at White-Sale time if you must get them new. Sheets can sometimes be found at estate auctions—or at the sales that occur when hostelries go out of business—for a fraction of their original cost. And there's nothing quite as easy on the epidermis as an *old* sheet. I think I've actually bought—for bed use—only two sheets in my life. I've often been given sheets, I've inherited them, and once I was awarded some for appearing on a television quiz show called "What's My Line?" If you have bought your sheets, you don't have to throw them away or demote them to dust rags when they've started wearing thin in the middle. Cut them in half, straight down the length in the middle, and then sew them together again with former outer edges seamed in the middle of the bed. That way you double the life of a sheet. If you're entranced with the idea of a fitted bottom sheet (and you lack enough of them), you can also transform a flat top sheet by stitching the corners.

Blankets, too—even electric ones—can be bought cheaply at auctions, secondhand shops, garage sales. Also, banks often offer them as premium gifts to lure you into opening an account. If secondhand blankets are a bit shabby, they can often be rendered "like-new" by replacing the ribbon edging from your fabric-scraps bag; or, convert them into quilts. You don't have to become a patchwork expert (though that's easy and fun—see page 67). Just whip up a blanket cover from some old set of curtains or a no-longer-worn housecoat. Figured or checked or striped on one side and a solid color on the other is attractive.

Ready-made bedspreads are an expensive indulgence, when it's *so* easy to buy lengths of fabric and sew them together. Here's how to make one easy bed-throw.

How to Make a Throw for a Double Head-Against-The-Wall Bed Out of Narrow-Width Fabric

Materials and Tools Needed:
eleven 2/3 yards 27-inch fabric
scissors
needle and thread (or a sewing machine)
straight pins

Directions:
1. Trim the two ends of the fabric so that it is exactly straight across (fabric is sometimes torn across in shops resulting in one edge being somewhat longer than the other).
2. Measure the length of fabric and divide its length by four.
3. Cut the fabric into four equal lengths.
4. Stitch (or hand sew) these four equal lengths together along their long sides, allowing 3/4-inch seams and making sure that you are seaming the fabric on the "wrong" side in each case.
5. Throw the spread on your bed, centering the centermost seam. You will find that the other two seams occur along the edges of the bed.
6. Cut off the two foot-of-bed corners in a curve.
7. Now "hang" the edges of the spread by pinning the fabric up all around at the height you want it to fall to.
8. Remove the throw from the bed and trim off excess fabric from the edges you have just pinned up.
9. Stitch (or hand sew) the hem all around the edge of the throw on the "wrong" side.

This type of bed throw is perfect for the springs-and-mattress set that sits right on the floor. It also works fine with a bed set up higher; but in that case you might want to use it as a coverlet in conjunction with a bed skirt or dust ruffle. A worn-out sheet or other

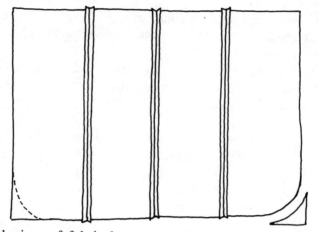

discarded piece of fabric between springs and mattress is the best foundation for a dust ruffle. Just sew it to this hidden piece of material at the edge of the bed all around, being sure that you have enough fabric for ruffling (one-third more than the perimeter of the bed) or for box-pleating at the corners (a yard more than the bed's perimeter).

The dust ruffle needn't be of the same fabric as the bedspread. In fact, you can get more decorative mileage out of the bed if it is of a contrasting color and/or material, perhaps matching the room's curtains, the wall color, or the slipcover on another piece of furniture. A large bed in a small bedroom is the dominant article of decor, so it pays to choose the fabric of the bedspread with great care. You can, and should, build the room's entire decoration scheme around the bedspread. If you have moved into a predetermined color scheme, take along samples of the colors you're stuck with when you go shopping for fabric.

Besides the homemade throw outlined above, there are a number of other easy bedspreads in your scrap bag or at your fingertips. How about one of the following:

a Mexican serape;

a fine lawn tablecloth left over from big dinner party days;

a bed sheet still too new to be comfortable for sleeping on;

full-length curtains that don't fit your new windows;

sewn-together bath mats;

a discarded fur coat, possibly in pieces, checkerboarded with squares of cloth or leather.

If you know how to crochet, some of the world's most beautiful bedspreads are available to you. Most issues of any women's magazine feature a pattern for one. The last such magazine I glanced at happened to feature an exquisite bedspread made of alternate stripes of crocheting and cross-stitch embroidery (which *any*one can do). And, if you know how to do patchwork quilting, this whole discussion of bed covers is academic because you doubtless already have all the beds in your house spread with lovely patchwork (which is turning up in the most sophisticated and modern bedrooms today).

There is a way to make a patchwork quilt right on the sewing machine that produces the effect of a handmade traditional quilt in about one-tenth of the time it would take you (working alone) to do it all by hand. The secret is to first select a block pattern, such as "Log Cabin." Divide it up into square units, which are themselves divided into square and oblong parts; cut cotton batting and plain cotton backing into units of the same size as each square patchwork unit. On each square patchwork unit first stitch down a small square piece in the middle, stitching right through batting and backing. Then you build out from the center to the edge, stitching each part down on the wrong side of the cotton and then flipping it over. The separate blocks are then stitched together (on the wrong side again),

the borders of plain fabric are added, and the quilt is finished—in a trice.

An even easier patchwork coverlet can be made by alternating stripes of some plain solid-color fabric (perhaps velour or plush for contrast) with stripes made up of large squares of the more traditional patchwork materials (cotton checks, polka dots, small figures) simply sewn together in a row. Omit the cotton batting and backing, and you can make a coverlet like the one pictured to be used as a bedspread only in a jiffy.

In a small sleeping room where the bed takes up much of the floor space, you can get a lot of decorative mileage out of a headboard. You can make one yourself by gluing a picture molding "frame" to the wall and letting it enclose an oblong piece of wallpaper or fabric that matches the fabric used on the bed, wall, or window; or use a solid-backed bookcase turned around with its front to the wall; or be playful with one of the following notions:

iron scrollwork from a dismantled fence or porch railing;
a snow fence picked up at a country auction;
the rugged wooden circle from one end of a cable spool;
four or five window blinds bolted together;
a striped awning hung from the ceiling to behind the bed's head;
a headboard-shaped "pillow" of 1-inch foam rubber covered in the same fabric as your bedspread and nailed at its top to the wall;
a panel of latticework.

Old fur coats can be very useful in bedrooms; and they can be picked up for just a few dollars in thrift shops. The only fur coats I've ever owned have been those shucked by friends and relatives who are less bleeding-heart than I am. (I prefer to let animals wear their own coats and let them die natural deaths.) After they've been worn for many seasons by others, fur coats in my hands wind up as throw pillows, footstool tops, or winter bedside rugs. Furlike fabric coats that have served their owners for some years can live much longer lives in this way, too. There's nothing quite like digging bare toes into some kind of warm pile as you swing out of bed on wintry mornings; the fur will dry out and crack less soon in this location, too, than it would spread out in the traditional manner in front of the wood-burning fireplace. Next to fur or fur-fabric, cotton pile or closely woven loop rugs are probably best in the bedroom. If the rugs

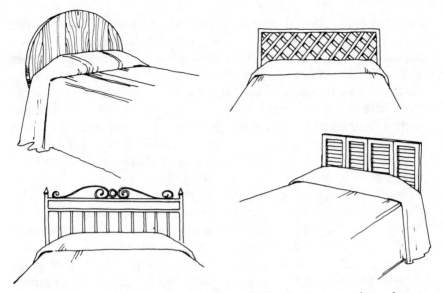

you're tired of in the bathroom don't suit the bedroom color scheme, dye them—cotton twist takes to home-dyeing superbly.

After the place to lay down your weary bones, the next most urgent piece of furniture for the sleeping room is usually the bureau or chest of drawers. A good, solid wooden chest with all its drawers intact and operable can run into a good hunk of cash, even secondhand. Bargains, however, are occasionally to be found in junk shops, particularly if the piece is missing a drawer or even drawer pulls (which you can fashion yourself from any number of materials—old doorknobs, for instance, or bits of rope), or has a marred top surface (which you will probably cover up, anyway, with a bureau scarf or a coat of paint).

But where is it written that the only container for sweaters and shirts and socks and underwear and pajamas is a four-drawer chest or ten-drawer chest-on-chest? With the semi-demise some years ago of the separate dining room as an institution, a lot of dining room furniture became available in secondhand shops. Chief among this furniture was the object known as a "buffet." Rather than the table linens and silverware this piece was designed to accommodate, clothing can very efficiently be held in it—that is, all the garments that don't require hanging. In place of the decanters of port and sherry on top can be jewelry cases and toiletries and pin cushions. In the best of these old relics there are shallow top drawers (for hose, undies, handkerchiefs, scarves), long deep bottom drawers (for shirts, blouses, and such), and in between a cabinet effect, where you can roll up and pile sweaters and jerseys and the like and see them all at a glance when you open the doors.

Should you by chance come upon a commodious bureau on the street with a drawer missing, don't pass it by as defective. You can insert a board and use the missing-drawer space for open shelving.

Vintaged dining room suites often included a "serving table," a tall one- or two-drawer piece that makes a dandy dressing table, if its legs are shortened a bit, or a writing desk.

One of the best-looking small bedrooms I have known (it happened to be in an apartment rich in closet space) employed as its "bureau" a small chestnut kneehole desk that had been liberated from the owner's college dormitory room. The advantage of the desk-become-bureau is that it functions as a dressing table, too. You can sit down to brush your hair, apply makeup, tie your tie, or whatever. If the room is very small, it helps to be able to slide the seat (a stool or nail keg would be good for this) clear underneath and out of the walking-by space while it's not in use.

In a tall, narrow bedroom (one with high ceilings but very little wall or floor space—the kind that abound in brownstone conversions), one of your best bets for a bureau substitute is a series of packing boxes that will slide underneath the bed. Some department and variety stores sell such boxes as blanket and bedding storage items. But, of course, they can be gotten free from all sorts of places— off the streets, from grocery stores and other emporia that need to throw out their delivery cartons constantly, from your office (storage file boxes are great for this, though they require a very high bedstead to fit under). Old, orphaned bureau or desk drawers are an easy item to pick up in dumps; they too can be slid under the bed to function as they used to in better days. (They won't scratch a wood floor if you take the time to soap their sliding surfaces once in a while.) This kind of ad hoc bureau arrangement, which forces us to get down on the knees, or, at least bend down and stretch some muscles, is very good for health and well-being.

In a diminutive sleeping room, wall shelves or bookcases can perform perfectly well as bureaus, thus allowing you to use clothing as "decoration." What could be more elegant than a stack of vari-colored jerseys, shirts, and blouses neatly folded on a white-painted shelf along one bedroom wall? Wicker baskets in interesting shapes on other shelves can hold more personal items and provide contrasting eye interest. Whether on a deep bottom shelf or on the floor underneath high-hung separate shelves, picnic baskets or hampers hold less decorative (and less often used) items of clothing.

I personally am a little bit nuts on the subject of wicker and basketry. Others are not as crazy about it as I am, with the result that they tend to throw baskets away when they have lost just one small bit of their fibers. If you share my predilection, that's when you gather them in—from sidewalks, dumps, incinerator rooms, and other refuse-collecting places—after they have acquired a good color from aging. The popped strand in a basket can be turned to the wall, or the space left can be filled in with ribbon or yarn or a strip of the same fabric that is used in some other way in the room. The lost wicker hinge of a clothes hamper can be replaced with matching twine or cord, and the hamper can hold blankets in the corner of the bedroom. String can form handles of a reed carrying bag or basket, which can then hold all manner of toiletry or dress items.

I once found discarded on a brownstone front stoop a perfect, beautiful, wicker hanging bird cage. Its only sin against humanity was that the removable tray inside had not been cleaned out since its occupant had deceased or flown the coop. I snatched it quickly, deposited the offending tray in the nearest trash bin, took it home, and scrubbed it with vinegar and water. Suspended from the ceiling of my then wee bedroom, it was a pleasure to behold. This happened so long ago that I have since forgotten what lived in the bird cage in my home—certainly not a bird—probably a green, leafy plant. But it might just as well have held handkerchiefs, scarves, hats, or gloves.

If you are just as crazy about leather, tin, or wood, who's to object? Put your socks and underwear into tin cookie boxes you have hand-painted. Scrape the labels off a cigar box and wax it for holding bow ties or handkerchiefs. Cover the carton your steam iron came in with scraps of leather, polka dot cotton, or plaid stick-on paper, and fill it with cosmetics or toiletries.

The boudoir chair, or "slipper chair" as it was sometimes called, seems to have gone the way of the buffet and serving table in most American homes today. Perhaps that's a good thing, at least from a penny-pinching point of view. In the small sleeping room there is no space for such a luxury item; it's redundant, too, as slippers are logically placed at the edge of the bed. If you're lucky enough to have a large bedroom, most likely the kind of chair you seek is one that fits the corner desk spot or a large armchair in which you can curl up with a good book. (In the latter case you'll need a good reading light. Learn how to make one that is both handsome and functional out of some plastic drainpipe and a dairy-foods container on page 131.)

If, when you've taken care of all the essential pieces of furniture, you still have some room in your sleeping quarters for seating, why not create some by rescuing an automobile seat from some old jalopy consigned to the junkyard? Automobile seats—the old-fashioned kind with a separate back piece—make dandy bedroom seats, particularly if you slipcover them in some incongruous sort of bedroomy fabric, such as floral chintz, or a tiny-checked gingham— one of those prints that matches your wallpaper. A stretch fabric is even easier. You don't need a sewing machine, only a hammer and a few tacks, to fashion a cover that goes around each of the two pieces and is hammered into place in a wrinkle-free manner. The bucket seat

from a defunct sports car would also make a good boudoir chair. If it seats comfortably in an automobile, why not in your bedroom? It might present a bit more of a challenge to your upholstering capabilities, but then the bucket seats might be in such good condition that you don't have to cover them at all. This last-mentioned sort of "chair" fits nicely under the sloping ceiling of an under-the-roof bedroom.

The desk or work table mentioned above reminds us of the other functions sleeping quarters often fill, such as the study, arts-and-crafts corner, or sitting room. In big, old country houses, where bedrooms often contain a fireplace, how cozy and pleasant is the effect of a chair or two by the fireside, suggesting evening nightcaps partaken there—or breakfast for that matter. The seats from your expiring "economy car" would do well there. So would chairs cut out of large-size barrels—the sort you sometimes still see in neighborhood stores, full of pickles, or in country stores or health food shops, holding the flours and grains. Only once in a while are they available to the assiduous town-dump comber. But should you discover one there, here's what you should do with it.

How to Make a Slipper Chair Out of a Pickle Barrel

Materials and Tools Needed:
one large-sized pickle barrel or hogshead
one round section of 3/4-inch board or plywood, with the same diameter as the widest part of the barrel
three or four L-shaped metal braces and the screws to match them
one circle of 2-inch foam rubber, the same size as the round board
one circle of fabric, 8 inches longer in diameter than the board
handful of upholstery tacks or a staple gun
saw
hammer
two or three 2-inch flat-headed nails

Directions:
1. Turn the barrel upside down. Locate the center of the barrel staves and saw off half of the staves around one-half of the barrel's circumference.
2. Remove the barrel bottom as well.

3. On what will be the underside of the round 3/4-inch board, mark the spots where you will screw on the metal braces and the screw holes as well.
4. Put the foam rubber on top of the round board and the fabric over the foam rubber.
5. Pull the fabric down tightly all around and staple or tack it to the underside of the board, skipping the locations of the braces and screws.
6. Make holes through the fabric where the screws will go.
7. Attach the L-shaped braces to the inside of the barrel so that their horizontal portions are level with the sawed-off edge of the staves.
8. Position the round seat so that braces and brace marks match.
9. Working from underneath the seat, screw the screws into the seat's bottom.
10. For extra reinforcement, pound a few nails around the still complete staves and into the edge of the seat.

Now that you are going to sit on a hogshead, you might think of making a dressing table or a bookcase or a bedside table out of an orange crate. Those splendid wooden containers aren't as easy to come by as they used to be. Remember when you could just go down to the corner store and bring home two orange crates for a dollhouse, kitchen storage bin, or record holder? Or, remember when you could pick up one of those sturdy wooden dairy delivery crates on the street or sidewalk? They function so well as modular wall units, or, painted in your favorite colors, can become everything from footstools to file boxes. The usual sources have dried up. In my neck of

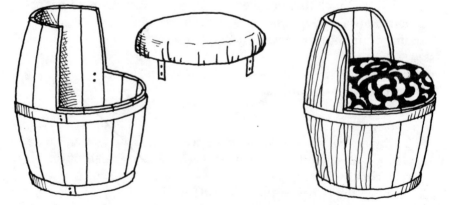

the woods the storekeepers burn them to heat their houses when the crates have finished their usefulness in the store. But a new manifestation has taken the place of the wooden milk, wine, or fruit crate. See page 137 for information.

Meanwhile, if the bedroom is big enough to boast some room for bookshelves, but the walls aren't strong enough to take the hammered-in kind of shelf braces, the good old brick-and-board method is probably still the best. Reserve the white bricks for the bedroom, and let the terra-cotta variety serve in other rooms. Usually, their earthy color goes better with living room and study color schemes. Glass bricks, of course, have a lighter effect, perhaps more suitable for the bedroom.

Due to family growth dining rooms and studies are often turned into bedrooms, or, rather, into sleeping rooms where other functions are also performed. The sewing room (once a standard in every middle class American home) all too frequently gives way to burgeoning life and becomes a nursery or bedroom. If these conversions happen in your home, take advantage of features that may be left over from the room's previous manifestation. The ex-dining room may have built-in drawer space or shelf space that can serve as your clothing chest; in the ex-study your shoes and/or hats can perform a decorative function on the shelf previously used for periodicals; the erstwhile sewing room may still be equipped with a pegboard that once held spools of thread, scissors, and the like. You can use that section of wall for hanging belts, beads, ribbons, ties, scarves, and so on.

Moving into a city apartment, a friend who solicited my decorating advice found a large dining room with a wooden wine cellar built into one wall. Being a teetotaler and preferring to dine at the end of the good-sized living room which was nearer the kitchen, my friend studied this wall for some weeks after she had converted the room into the master bedroom. When I saw the wine rack, inspiration struck me immediately. Since the (new) master bedroom was also the room with the right natural light, where my friend practiced her hobby of needlepoint, it was obvious: into each cutout hole, formerly occupied by a wine bottle on its side, we stuffed an empty, topless tin can or plastic food container; into each of these was put a different color of needlepoint yarn or a roll of canvas. The once wine-cellar became both a storage place for all her working materials and one of the most handsome decorative elements I've ever seen in a city apartment. My friend needed no interior designer to tell her that functionality and beauty are not antithetical.

Another dining-room-become-bedroom I have known presented to its new occupant the problem of "the room with too many windows and doors." There simply was no unbroken wall to provide head space for a double bed. Well, who said a bed *has* to lean against a wall? Obviously, the bed goes where the dining table used to go— where else, but in the middle of the room? A light fixture hung from the ceiling with a round Tiffany glass lampshade left behind to gladden this couple's antique-hunting hearts. It was this relic that suggested to us how to solve the bed space problem. Instead of a double-size mattress-and-springs set in the middle of the squarish room, why not a round bed? And a large, round water bed it was . . . and is. The water bed fit the room's proportions much better than the usual oblong bed would and didn't cost all that much because they were able to "get it wholesale." A small steamer trunk with its panels painted the same light blue of the walls held bedding and served as a bedside table. The only other object in the door-crazy room was a wicker wastebasket that had been found thrown away on the sidewalk in front of the building, holding a large Ficus plant. The plant's height provided a contrast with the lowness of the rest of the furnishings.

Which reminds me that some people fear decorating their sleeping quarters with plants. I don't know the origin of this prejudice— probably noticing nurses removing all the plants and flowers from hospital rooms at bedtime. I've never known why this is done, especially since plants exhale oxygen and inhale carbon dioxide, which is just the opposite of what people do. You'd think it would be a perfect symbiotic arrangement for plants and animals to sleep together. I personally have never thought a sleeping room quite complete without either a bouquet of fresh flowers or a potted plant or two. If the bedroom doesn't afford quite enough sunlight for the well-being of your plant, then put *that* plant in a sunny parlor window and choose shade-loving plants, such as Dracaena, ferns, and some kinds of begonia for the bedroom. But don't for the sake of any Old Wives' Tale leave growing green things out of your sleeping quarters.

If you can't afford the prices in the local greenhouse or plant store, then bum a "slip" from a friend who is trimming back his ivy or aspidistra. Rescue a purple passion plant from a garbage can; or find a post-holiday-time azalea discarded in your apartment building corridor. But don't neglect the inexpensive decorative note that a plant can provide. It's far less trouble to keep in beautiful condition than, for example, is sterling silver.

Should you share living quarters with a plant-eating cat, don't, please, fall for the plastic flower temptation. The only time for plastic flowers, in my opinion, is the middle of a cold, cold winter; and the only place for them is in the bathroom, alongside the snake plant. But more of that in Chapter 4.

Window treatments in a sleeping room can be frustrating or fun, depending on the window, the rest of the room's decoration, and your notion of fun. If your bedroom is fluffy feminine, with yards of marquisette or voile dust-ruffling the bed or skirting the dressing table, then you may want to be a bit more tailored in curtaining the window, lest the room resemble a giant powder puff. Straight fiberglass curtains from window top to floor are restful to the eye. A drawstring curtain rod allows you to filter the sunlight during the day and let optimum air in at night. If, on the other hand, the room is low key and clean of line, you may want to use the windows as a major focal point. Try "treating" them in one of the following ways:

   window shades striped with sticky-back tape in the colors of the
      room's color scheme;
   ceiling-to-floor drapes in a checked fabric on swing-away curtain
      rods that meet in the middle at night;
   a single tie-back curtain in a shocking color (let it be the only in-
      stance of that hue in the room) that is fixed across the top of
      the window and tied back to one side;
   louvres with frames and slats painted in contrasting colors;
   an old window screen into which you have woven strands of gaily
      colored yarn;
   glass beads fixed to wooden poles across the top and bottom of
      the window.

Also check out the window treatments outlined in Chapter 8.

If the room for sleeping, as is so often the case, is also someone's study, then you may want a room divider of some kind. No problem if the room is large enough: see Chapter 6 for how to construct a couple of easy folding screens. Where space is at a premium, however, you don't want to waste any of it by throwing away the foot or two of floor space that a folding screen needs to spread out and stand on. A tall, solid bookcase does it, of course, with the flat side acting as a wall or headboard to position your bed or other strong piece of furniture against. So does a drapery track fixed in the ceiling, with a curtain, bedspread, or rug hung from it. If your ceiling can take this degree of weight, even a wide venetian blind can do the job. Still better than the venetian blind with wood or metal or plastic slats, is the matchstick roll-up blind. People have a tendency to discard these versatile blinds—when they get a little splintery, I guess—and they can often be picked up from dumps or sidewalks only slightly used. The sidewalk is where I found a whole set of matchstick roll-up blinds in different sizes. They served me well for years as blinds on living room windows, as wrap-around bathroom sink bottoms to hide the plumbing, and as wall covering in a room that needed relief from all-white walls, where they held pin-up lamps and decorative hangings.

If your ceiling plaster is a bit ancient and not too firm, you may find a better room divider is something that doesn't depend on the ceiling. Try putting up a couple of spring tension poles. They won't pull it down and may even help hold *up* the ceiling. Wrap a length of wide fabric around and between the poles and sew it together. I once wrapped some matchstick blinds around an old tubular iron gate I'd found abandoned in a neighbor's chicken yard and used that for a room-divider–headboard held upright on its side. The bed propped it on one side and the long table–desk where my husband worked held it up on the other. It worked well and looked neat in an offbeat way. There was even a part of a hinge left on the ex-gate to which I was able to attach a homemade lamp for reading in bed.

A word about light and color for sleeping rooms. When I first acquired a home of my own that wasn't a "furnished room," dark decorator colors were *in*, for any sort of room, with the possible exception of the bathroom and kitchen. The two rooms that made up that apartment—both the living room with Pullman kitchen in one corner and the second small room—were painted in deep, dark opaque green, a sort of bottom-of-the-ocean color. There was little enough light seeping into this basement (excuse me, this "ground floor") flat in any case, and the green did nothing to encourage or reflect it. Rather than stylish, it was just plain dismal. I had neither the time nor the cash to transform the big room with the (at least) two coats of light-colored paint that would have been required to cover that stygian darkness or I would have. The landlord, naturally, would not. After I had lived there for two-plus years, however, he was persuaded to paint the small room—the bedroom—a bright canary yellow. You have no idea the difference this made to my psyche! Opening my eyes in the morning, I felt far happier when all that sunshine color greeted me, rather than the dark wet-leaf shade that had been there before. It was really a mood elevator. Now, some folks object to having their moods elevated first thing upon rising. Maybe for them a chocolate brown, deep purple, or even ebony black bedroom is just what the doctor ordered: it may even contribute to their sense of security to reproduce a womblike atmosphere where they sleep. Okay, lay on the dark paint. Others go for absolute neutrality—all beiges, whites, and off-whites—in the boudoir; it seems a good contrast with the hectic quality of their outside lives. Leaving all that intense work or other activity behind and entering the sanctum sanctorum, they just want the utmost calm in coloring to prevail in the bedroom. No boudoir wall color is verboten any more, so suit your personality type and taste preferences.

If you're stuck with some eternal bedroom furniture, however, be sure its coloring will harmonize with the color you're contemplating for the walls. The only sure way to do this is to bring paint samples home from the paint store and try them against your furniture, drapes, or whatever, one by one, in both daytime and nighttime, under natural and then artificial light. Then buy your paint, not before. If you've never done this before, the astonishing variety of shades of paint in *one color* will amaze you (and some of their names will, too).

Should you chance to find a leftover partial roll of wallpaper don't destroy it. (People are always over-ordering wallpaper because most papers can't be bought by the foot or yard, but must be ordered by the roll.) Hold it up against your bedroom wall; one wall may be able to "take" wallpaper in a pattern (it may even need it to impose some stability on the plaster). Then you can save money on the paint necessary for the other walls—match it to one of the colors in the "found" wallcovering. Or, you may want to use the paper to treat windows or door, cutting strips of it to frame door or window. Or, cut shapes out of the wallpaper to create designs on the wall, perhaps to suggest a headboard above the bed.

If the wall you paper doesn't swallow up quite all of the partial roll, you may want to use it to:

line shelves or drawers;

cover a wastebasket;

tart up a lampshade;

cover a lamp base;

renew window shades by covering the part pulled down during
the daytime;

put a piece under the glass top of your bedside table.

Some of these devices will serve to pull the room together, re-
minding the viewer of the opposite wall. The only thing *not* to do
with bits of remnant wallpaper is throw it away. It's too expensive
to waste. Hold it for a while after its parent has gone onto your wall.
You'll find a use for it, even if it's only for gift wrapping. The same
admonition applies to the pages of especially decorative calendars.
Many of my friends and family have received gifts of books and
other essentials encased in May, June, or July, in a lovely Japanese-
print-like calendar page. No one seems to mind.

With only one or two bedroom walls patterned, and the others a
plain background, you can hang in the bedroom photographs, mem-
orabilia, or "art work." Don't let anyone dictate to you the sort of
painting, print, or photograph that is appropriate to the bedroom—
with one exception. Never leave on the wall (or bureau) a photograph
of a person who no longer means anything to you, even if he or she
is very good-looking indeed—a sure way to disturb your repose.
Don't ever hang a picture simply because it "goes with the color
scheme," if you don't fancy it. The bedroom is the place where you
can pamper your predilection for "pretty" things, which can be very
soporific. Think about hanging these things on the bedroom walls:

a very traditional watercolor of fruits—pears, peaches, grapes,
strawberries;

a Chinese string bag macraméed in a pleasant diamond pattern;

a finely designed square of fabric, such as a scarf;

your collection of hats, necklaces, or other decorative wearing
apparel;

Christmas tree ornaments and trimmings;

a rope ladder, suspended from the ceiling, which you can decorate with beads, belts, sunglasses and such.

Mirrors, without which no sleeping–dressing room should be,
can in themselves be a wonderful decorative effect. You've heard,
until it's come out your ears, how mirrors (or mirroring attached
directly to the wall) push the walls out and make a small room seem

larger. And they do. Anyone who has walked right into a mirror in a restaurant, while aiming for that small unoccupied table "on the far side of the room," can attest to that. So, if wide, open space is what you want for your bedroom, cover one wall, part of one wall, or a door with a mirror or mirroring, which is now relatively inexpensive and is produced in squares that even the most inept amateur can apply himself.

A mirror, whether hanging on the wall, leaning on the wall from the mantelpiece, or positioned over the dressing table or bureau, is definitely a part of most bedrooms. You can have fun with a bedroom mirror. You may want to embellish the plain frame it came in. Think about a mirror framed in some of the following ways. Starting with a boudoir mirror (of about 11 by 15 inches) in a cheap wooden frame:

glue corkboard to the wood (it can then double for a pincushion or bulletin board);

glue to the wood a super-frame of cardboard covered in scraps of the fabric used in drapes or bedcovers;

nail over the already existing frame an old-fashioned, ornate picture frame;

glue to the frame a profusion of seashells, decorative buttons, rosettes of gift wrapping ribbon, or halved walnut and/or peanut shells;

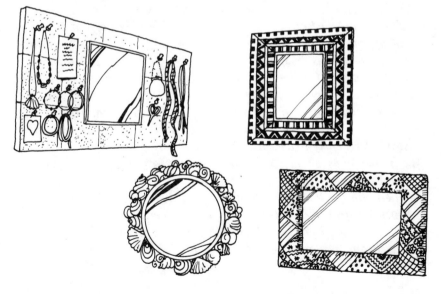

cover the wooden frame with a pair of those fishnet stockings left
over from the fifties;

glue gangs of interestingly shaped uncooked pasta (bowties,
shells, wheels, etc.) to the frame and then gild over it;

cover the frame in patchwork quilting.

Rooms for sleeping and rooms for washing are sometimes one
and the same, but usually only in hotel rooms in Europe, where older
houses sensibly separate the washbasin from the toilet. In some avant-
garde American homes a bathtub is occasionally inserted in the bedroom, an interior-designer conceit that still needs justifying to me.
In those home decorating magazines where I've noticed this odd
combination, it is always a feature of a Southwestern home. At any
rate, taking a bath in the bedroom is far removed from the penny-
pinching philosophy. So on we go in the next chapter to the bathing
proposition—into the next room.

Tips

- *Lamps for bedrooms can afford to be less classic, more frivolous
than in other rooms. Try covering a lampshade with a small-
unit patchwork, or even with a sun hat. The one I sewed together
out of scraps of this and that found its perfect home as the shade
for a bedside lamp.*
- *Plywood can be bought from lumber dealers, either cut to your
specifications or in the 4- × 8-foot sheets in which it is manufactured. It comes in widths of 1/4 inch, 3/8 inch, 1/2 inch, 5/8
inch, and 1 1/4 inches and in different grades of quality, as well.*
- *Staple guns, which may seem superfluous until you really get into
home-decorating, are essential, multifunctional machines.
Watch for a sale in a paint, flooring, and wall covering supplies
store. I recently priced one at only $4.50!*
- *Wallpaper goes on sale, too, often just before a new sample book
comes out, as does flooring material. I suppose this happens
when the particular pattern is being discontinued or when the
store has found that the material has been overproduced.*
- *A squeeze-tube item called Liquid Steel is an indispensable aid to
the home decorator—it's especially useful in working with
stained glass, as it looks like leading.*

- *If you don't have rubber or plastic rug linings for all your floor coverings—those mats that go underneath and hold them in place, thus saving you from a lawsuit from a visiting bone breaker—there is a latex coating you can buy. Just brush it onto the underside of your rug, be it secondhand sisal, brand-new wool pile, or handmade braid.*
- *When shopping for decorating fabrics, don't neglect the dress-goods shops or departments. Fabrics intended for clothing are often some of the best materials for upholstering, slipcovering, or drapery and are often bought cheaper under the "dressmaking" sign.*

4

Bathing Room

According to some people, who must be either immensely large or formidably clean, there is hardly enough room for bathing in the Atlantic and Pacific Oceans combined. But, being a moderately hygienic person who happens to have moved recently into a house with the world's tiniest bathroom, let me say this: if your bathroom is small, count your lucky stars, especially if its minisculity means more space in the other, walk-around-in rooms. After all, what do you need with wide, open spaces in the baño, which is easier to heat in winter if it's postage-stamp size.

The other questionable feature of my bathing room is that the toilet and sink seem to be very low down, close to the floor. Possibly the fixtures, which I inherited with the rest of the house, were installed for children—or very short people. To correct this defect would doubtless cost an arm and a leg in plumber's and/or carpenter's fees, so I'll content myself with advising any of you who are at the point of creating a bathroom in attic, cellar, or hall closet, that toilet fixtures do come in all sizes—short or tall, fat or skinny. Your own personal dimensions can be accommodated nicely (and comfortably) at the beginning of things. You don't *need* to bend over double every time you wash your hands, nor should you doubt you will ever get up again when you sit down on the throne.

Bathtubs, to move on to a more esthetically pleasing aspect of the subject, come in all sizes and shapes, too. If the minute area you're contemplating turning into a complete bathroom boasts no 8-foot-long wall, why not fit in a square tub, rather than a coffin-shaped one? You'll probably never have to bed down in it, and if it's deep enough you can dunk just as much of yourself as in the full-length variety.

Why not do without a bathtub entirely and install a shower only? Stall showers now come in many interesting materials. Fiberglass and other plastics are far more waterproof than the old standard four-sided tin (or other metal) boxes. Those usually manage to spring a leak at one of the bottom corners before you've had them six months, thus ruining your living room ceiling.

Should you be faced with the problem of fitting bathroom fixtures into an oddly shaped space, remember that there is more than one way to arrange them. A square tub in the middle of a room, for instance, or either sink or water closet in a corner. Yes, they do come in triangular shapes that fit into corners or under staircases or eaves.

Ceramic tile, of course, is still probably the most desirable material for bathroom walls, floors, and even ceilings. Tiling around certain parts of the room (the most moist parts) can sometimes be accomplished with the tiles left over from a recent tiling job and, hence, thrown away in the dump, abandoned on a sidewalk, or stacked in the corner of a basement, awaiting your eagle eye. Linoleum squares can also be a good waterproofer (whether actually linoleum, or vinyl or whatnot) and can be easily cut to fit wherever you want them to go. After laying them on the floor of your bathroom, why not simply carry the same material up over the walls, at least halfway up, behind your toilet, sink, and/or bathtub–shower? With any such piece-by-piece arrangement the secret is close fit, secure gluing or sealing, and ample caulking between the units, especially with tiles.

Unsightly plumbing—though it happens in other rooms as well— is most often a problem in bathrooms. You can either conceal it, or you can make use of it—play it up. By conceal, I don't mean anything Victorian such as hiding the "water closet" inside a cane-seated chair or throne effect. (How silly can you get?) But those pipes, without which you can neither run yourself a wash *nor* flush the toilet, are usually just not very attractive objects. Happily, they are often located where they can be hidden from sight, if not by the porcelain (or plastic) of the fixture itself, then by some screening made of metal, fabric, wood, or plastic. A drainpipe, water pipe, or heating pipe that goes right smack through the corner of your room, ceiling to floor, will be a lot less noticeable if you paint it the same color as the walls around it. If the walls are papered, cold-water pipes can seem to recede into the walls, when wrapped with a bit of the same covering you have on the walls. If it's regular wall*paper*, better not try it with heat or hot-water ducts. But, if it's vinyl or fabric, why not?

"Playing them up" means candy-striping the pipes or ducts with contrasting colors of sticky tape for a circus or barbershop effect— not too bizarre for a bathroom; winding them maypole-style with strips of fabric; even twining pipes with plastic flowers is the one permissible use for those artifacts. Plastic flowers, in my opinion, were *made* for baths, whether blooming from decorative baskets, wound around utilitarian ducts of one sort or another, or ganged up in boxes on top shelves (farther up than the shampoo and bath towels).

Though its function is a very utilitarian one, and great reaches of space aren't really desirable in your run-of-the-mill bathroom, there's no reason why it should just be skipped over when it comes to making your living place handsome. Even a small bath usually has room for a plant or two, and some plants take very well to the steamy atmosphere. Snake plants are not the only greenery that like moist air to live in. Try several varieties of ferns, some African violets, a dracena, or Hawaiian ti plant. Hang your Swedish ivy there or Wandering Jew. Set on the tile an Aphelandra or gloxinia. Any of these plants will rejoice in the frequent running of bath or shower water and can live in close proximity to wet rubber shower curtains.

It has always seemed to me that not only some species of flora, but of fauna as well, belong properly in bathrooms. If you have an extra unused tub, why not turn it into an aquarium? Goldfish are just as pleasurably viewed from the top as from the side. You may prefer to turn the extra tub into a terrarium or huge planter. Small boys' pet turtles, lizards, and newts have historically found natural habitats in bathrooms. Use them as decoration there. Use anything live rather

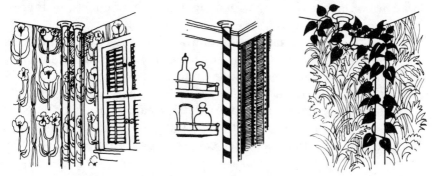

than the odious prurient-interest sketches or photographs some people think "belong" in the bathroom.

One of the nice things about the room where you bathe is that so many items that actually do belong in it make such suitable decoration. If you have pinched a lot of pennies by making up your own cosmetics and toiletries, show off their tints and shades in a set of canning jars. They look fine. Bars of soap in various colors and shapes or all alike, for that matter, in a clear glass vase or large brandy snifter are handsome. Soaps in the form and colors of lemons, oranges, and strawberries in a white porcelain saucer beside the bathroom washbowl may never be used up on dirty hands. And don't underestimate the decorative value of towels and face cloths. Neat stacks of these necessary accoutrements on open shelves give off a splendidly opulent feeling.

Wicker objects seem to have a natural affinity for bathrooms; the moist atmosphere probably prolongs their lives, too. Shelves, wastebaskets, tissue dispensers, and flowerpots of wicker go well there. So do representations of animals—bas reliefs on the walls, statuary on the floor, ceramic models on bathtub ledges. Put your collection of model frogs, owls, or sea horses in the bathing place. Your accumulation of large seashells will find an appropriate home there, too.

I had an aunt who, when she wasn't using it in the dining-room-turned-into-sewing-center, let her portly dressmaker's form stand in an unused corner of the bathroom. As a small girl it gave me a comfortable, secure feeling to see it there. These matronly figures, incidentally, have become decorator's items in recent years and are often placed around apartments where no one *ever* makes a dress— for purely decorative effect. Sometimes they are draped with striking swatches of fabric, or hung with dangling beads or chains, or topped with a colorful floppy hat.

One of the most versatile of utilitarian-decorative, natural objects for the bathroom is the natural sponge or the Loofah. If you live near a free source of these picturesque animals, lucky you are. Gather a group in various sizes and let them live in (or alongside) your bathtub. Or suspend them over it in a colorful string bag. Those of us who are not seaside dwellers must buy the real thing, or make do with manufactured sponges. But the latter can be a pretty touch of color by

tubside, too. Pile them in an open-top, clear plastic box through which their hues can show.

Stones, too, make good "natural" decoration for bathrooms, and certain stones can even be useful. A pumice stone is good for polishing the bottoms of feet, knees, and elbows, reducing calluses or removing paint stains from the skin. Small, round pebbles in a sauce dish make an excellent soap holder and drainer, saving you a pretty penny on what might otherwise be wasted soap; playing-marbles in the bottom of a dish can perform the same function. Either of these arrangements saves you the ugliness of one of those plastic soap drainers the Fuller brush man leaves when he calls on you. In my part of the world natural garnets and other semiprecious stones can be picked up off dirt roads near an old iron mine. These make good drain bottoms for soap dishes, too. And a perfectly shaped "crystal" of some ferrous stone found in the woods is, for me, a window-sash ornament in winter.

Photographs (under glass of course, or, if not glassed in, then covered with some preservative and anticurling coating such as shellac) look good in bathrooms. But, if the bath is the place where the photos that you wouldn't keep anywhere else wind up, it's better to consign them to the trash bin. Even in the lavatory, only snapshots of people, places, or objects you really want to go on looking at should be displayed. Better to cover that tiny bit of wall space with playing cards. Glue them on and cover them with a coat of varnish, shellac, or polyurethane.

Among academics, the bathroom or guest lavatory seems to be the place to hang framed degree certificates. Personal letters from the famous or eccentric (preserved under glass) are not inappropriate on the bathroom wall. Or paper it with one of the following:

sheet music no longer in your repertory;

especially attractive magazine covers;

well-printed performance programs or menus from meals you have enjoyed;

antique posters or advertising art.

Contemporary posters, which also make good bathroom wall-papering, can be had free from a number of businesses with clever solicitation. Once when I was teaching at an art institute I canvassed the airlines for a collection of their posters "for classroom use." Result: a bathroom papered with as glorious a collection of art as I'd seen in a lavatory in a long time. My favorite was a giraffe's neck and head made of flags of different countries against an electric blue background. Thank you again, Air France.

In a book called *The Catalog of Free Things* by Feinman and Weiss (William Morrow, 1976) I learned that Lufthansa German Airlines, 1640 Hempstead Turnpike, East Meadow, New York 11554, will send you free (you're not even asked for 50 cents to cover cost of mailing) a Pop Art poster for your bathroom wall. This book, incidentally, is far superior for the home decorator to the old standby *1001 Valuable Things You Can Get Free* by Weisinger, now in its tenth edition. The latter volume seems to have become largely a listing of the free literature and catalogs you can get from here and there. Some of these, of course, are worth having. Even when pushing their products, a number of manufacturers of home construction, repair, upkeep, and decoration materials do a good job of giving advice about various processes, materials, and tools of interest to anyone attempting to keep his home in good shape and not lose his shirt in the process.

If you're of an economical turn of mind, whether it's money, string, or the environment, a good way to save water in the bathroom is not to use so much in flushing the john. For about 7 dollars you can buy a little polypropylene plastic doohickey (called The Saveit) to install in the toilet tank; it automatically reduces the amount of water stored there and available for flushing. But, obviously, anything that stops the refilling water from running into the tank sooner will do it. Bending the float rod will accomplish this in a small way; dropping a couple of bricks or stones into the tank will produce the same effect as The Saveit, which in its advertising guarantees to save you about 500 gallons of water per month.

You may have thought that tank tops and covers of fabric are a bit of an affectation, but actually they are useful and preservative. These "sweaters" for the toilet absorb the moisture that forms on the tank so it doesn't drip on the floor, form puddles, and go through the floor to make stains on the ceiling of the room below. They are a good means also of lending a note of cheerful color to an otherwise drab room. If your bathroom has all white fixtures—a black-and-white checked floor (for example), white tile, and plaster walls and ceiling— a flick-of-the-wrist decorating accent could be an all-fireman-red toilet seat cover and tank sweater. It would do a lot to warm up the bathroom on a cold morning. This pair of furnishings could very easily be made out of cotton loop or terry cloth or an old bathrobe that has seen better days; and with the sleeves you could make a matching bath mat.

If next to the toilet fixture you have some space you don't know what to do with, how about adding to your bathroom a bidet? The bidet is still too seldom seen in bathrooms on this side of the Atlantic; I've often wondered why. If you are fortunate enough to move into a bathroom that has one, and you consider it an excess, you can always use it for a foot bath or a planter. Should the opposite be your problem, you may want to consider installing a composting toilet. This fairly new product doesn't flush waste down into pipes but holds it instead and turns it by chemical means into excellent fertilizer for your garden. You can find a particularly good-looking one, called The Ecolet, advertised now in countless outdoor or home magazines.

Somewhere within easy reach of the toilet is toilet tissue, either in pastel shades that contribute to the room's color scheme or in utilitarian white. (I've often wondered, in these days of high consciousness with regard to bleaches and dyes and their effect on the biosphere, why toilet tissue isn't manufactured in unbleached "natural," haven't you?) If there isn't a built-in tissue dispenser in the tile or wall of your bath, consider containing the tissue in one of the following ways:

> a piece of cord or rope (macraméed, if you like) passed through the roll and over some architectural feature like the shower curtain rail or a wall hook;
> a wire coat hanger;

a bunch of key chains or light pulls fastened together;

a length of rawhide or a narrow belt;

a wicker (there it is again) basket or dispenser;

a terra-cotta flowerpot atop the water tank.

If you have moved into an older dwelling with an old-fashioned, slope-backed clawfoot bathtub, you don't have to get a carpenter to build an enclosure around it; these picturesque old tubs are very "in" now. Scrape the outside smooth (the part that shows to the unbathing eye), paint it your favorite bathroom color, and enjoy the fact that you'll be able to clean under it with ease. Should the inside enamel in the tub, and other bathroom fixtures for that matter, be chipped here and there, rather than doing an imperfect patching job with an unsatisfactory product (enamel, which doesn't work very well, and never matches anyway), how about buying a $2.49 package of clever little waterproof decals called Shower Flowers? Create a witty design of daisies to cover the imperfections. Matching the length of your bathtub, or in a circular daisy chain on your shower floor, these decals can save you a nasty fall as well.

Should the medicine cabinet over the washbasin be missing its glass shelves, you can save money (and frustration—they may not be making glass shelves in that particular size any more) by replacing the shelves with thin pieces of wood picked up from a nearby sidewalk, trash pile, or dump. Discarded shingles, split to the right width, work very well in the medicine cabinet.

If, on the other hand, an *extra* medicine cabinet is in your windfall, bear in mind that it will make an excellent spice cabinet for the kitchen. If there is none at all in the new bathroom, consider keeping all your medicines in the hall linen closet or the top drawer of your bedroom bureau. Then you'll be able to hang some other kind of mirror over the bathroom sink. How about one framed in an old gingerbread picture frame, or one of the ways mentioned in Chapter 3.

If the bathroom mirror is your dressing, shaving, making-up reference, it will pay to have adequate lighting on it. Leave the 20-watt bulb in the ceiling of the room, but put a stronger one in the light that illuminates the mirror. Theatrical lights around the mirror are effective. If you can't manage that, however, perhaps you can afford a string of exterior Christmas tree lights. Festoon the mirror with the

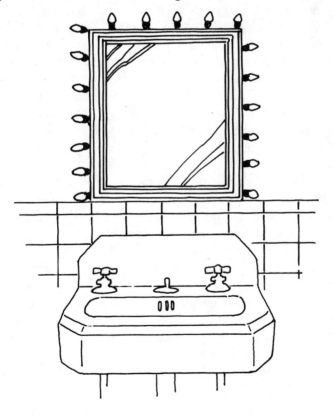

wires and insert uncolored bulbs of the highest wattage the fixture will take.

Should the glass in this same inherited bath also have disappeared from the sliding panels or doors that close off the "water closet," or keep the shower water from flooding the floor, I suggest replacing it with Plexiglass. It is cheaper to buy, simpler to install, easier to keep clean, and next to impossible to shatter. It also comes, like real glass, in various degrees of opacity as well as a wide variety of colors.

Dressing a bathroom window can sometimes be combined with handling the shower curtain question. Bathroom windows, when they exist at all (windowless baths are the rule, rather than the exception, in most middle class apartments), seldom need curtaining. For privacy frosted glass, ordinary window shades, or movable-slat shutters are ideal. In a small room slats should repeat the color of the wall paint, or shades the pattern of the wallpaper, to create the illusion of more space. If one wall supports both a window and the long side of the tub, you can kill two birds with one stone: put a curtain rod or spring tension pole clear across the wall at window-top level and hang a shower curtain on it. This hanging will do double duty as window curtain and shower curtain—drawn across the window when you're showering, pulled to the side of the window when you're not. You will need another curtain for the other side of the tub, but it needn't match the window one (that plain, neutral-colored plastic one you brought from your last bathroom will do). Make the curtain of a beautiful "decorator" waterproof fabric, and it will be the focal point of the room.

I once solved the window dressing problems of a long, narrow one-window-at-the-end bathroom in a cold climate in a rather unorthodox way that pleased the owner, provided additional insulation, and tickled my sense of fun, all in one. The inhabitant of the house, a collector of Medieval art, had hung two oil paintings of some royal personages on the long bathroom wall opposite the bathtub. The tub area, which was also the location of the shower head, was fitted out with an L-shaped shower curtain rod. I made for both window and tub a pair of rich purple velour drapes, caught back with tie-backs of golden tasseled cord. Both sets of drapes had under them an ecru curtain of waterproof plastic, which kept the shower water *in*side the tub and the wintry breezes *out*side the window when showering was going on. A Chinese rug in tones of purple, red, and gold—as much as my sense of the absurd—actually dictated the color scheme. And when I sewed pairs of gold crowns of lamé into the royal purple of the curtains, my "client" was as pleased as punch.

If, like mine, your shower curtains are other people's castoffs, you may have acquired them minus shower curtain rings. These little keyhole-shaped pieces of hardware can easily be fashioned from large-size paper clips by wielding a pair of pliers; or clip-on window curtain hangers, which are very inexpensive, can be used instead.

A bathroom problem that besets the moist-climate dweller who hasn't an automatic clothes dryer in the basement is how to get bathing towels dry without a sunny window or windy weather. Here again the small bathroom is an advantage. It heats up quickly and uses less wattage with a small space heater, which will also dry the towels. So will a wonderful invention that you can have built into the bathroom or buy freestanding: towel racks with a heating coil inside them. Just hang up your towels, plug it in, and they're dry in a trice. The freestanding kind can be stored in a closet when not needed. They're very expensive, but in some climes worth it.

One of the problems of the too-small bathroom is too many doors for comfort and convenience. See if you can't eliminate a door or two. Possibly the entrance door can do double duty, as in a bathroom I "treated" recently. When the entrance door is shut, the linen closet (in the bathroom) is exposed; when the entrance door swings open, it closes off the linen closet. Similarly, in another bath—miniscule lavatory, actually—the closed entrance door exposes the toilet stall portion of the room, but when the door is open it closes off the toilet. In each case there had originally been two doors getting in each other's way and using up almost nonexistent space in the room.

Except for the matter of quick heating, the problem of the too-spacious bathroom isn't a problem at all. But if it seems to you that combining dressing room and bathroom isn't a solution to the yawning square feet across the room from the tub and shower, you might consider moving in a wicker or overstuffed chaise longue. Cover it with toweling and do your sun-lamp bathing there; or leave it as it is and turn that corner of the bathing room into a cozy reading corner; or just quietly faint there from time to time.

This seems to have been just about enough time to spend on the bath, which is in many ways the least problematical room in the house in that its "furniture" you're usually stuck with. If not, and you have

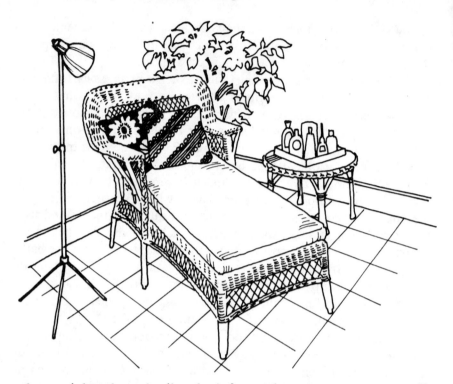

to buy a sink, tub, and toilet, don't forget that you can save yourself
a small fortune by getting these fixtures secondhand. Also, remember
that you can lend a custom look to your baño if sink, tub, and toilet
don't "match" with regard to period, color, or manufacturer.

In conclusion I'd like to share with you a dream I've long cherished
of a bathroom incomparable. It is a medium-sized room done in what
the decorators like to call "earth colors." The fixtures are all beige
enamel and tile; standard chrome faucets have been replaced with
gold-colored hardware. The walls are rough wood panels that have
weathered to a good sandy tone, except for one, which is covered
with grass cloth. The large, thirsty bath towels piled everywhere are
striped of loamy dark brown and terra-cotta orange. The single window is curtained in a patchwork glazed chintz, which is used for the
ceiling covering, as well. The patchwork pattern repeats the autumnal
colors with a bit of green thrown in. And the rest of the "decoration"
is green-leaved plants in handsome deep brown baskets. It's a charming bathroom, but not one that my own little closet for pygmies is
destined to become. Perhaps you will find an idea or two in it for your
place of bathing.

TIPS

- *If your bath towels or face cloths, having attained a ripe old age, aren't as opulently "thirsty" as they once were, stitching two together back to back is a good idea. Or reverse the towels, as you did the aged sheets (see page 64), and seam down the middle. Or turn old bath towels into new hand towels or face cloths. A double turkish towel soaks up more than a single, going-thread-bare one. Better still, is a flannelette lining in between. Such a towel will take longer to dry out, but it will feel better to the post-bather in the winter or in a rainy climate. .*
- *Household sponges should be cleaned from time to time by soaking in cold water with a little vinegar.*
- *A discarded wooden toilet seat, sterilized by scrubbing with hot water and soap and then sanded and waxed or painted, makes an excellent picture- or mirror-frame for the bathroom.*
- *Plumbing supplies can be bought at cut-rate prices if you know where to go. Often it's a store that also carries cut-rate drugs and hardware.*

5

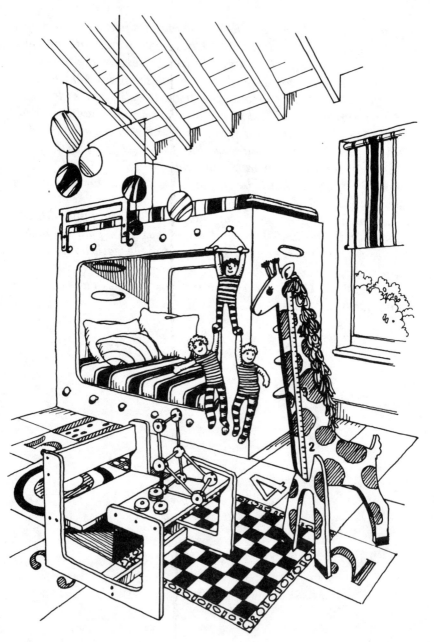

Room for Little People

A new baby can create havoc with the decoration of living quarters. Doubtless that's the reason couples start looking for a more spacious apartment or house the instant they learn of the pregnancy. A prudent plan; but if you're stuck with the two rooms plus kitchenette for a while, there's no reason why Little Stranger should disturb your carefully worked out decor, taking over the whole shooting match with his/her diaper pail, potty-chair, carriage, stroller, high chair, crib, bathinette, and all manner of equipment.

Yes, a newborn babe does need a place to sleep of his very own: that's what he spends a large proportion of his first year doing. A huge crib, however, is not necessary or even desirable from the infant's point of view for some months. You know that Early American or Shaker cradle next to the fireplace, where you keep the firewood? Put Baby in that; it was, after all, made for precisely this purpose. Other things that you might convert into a bassinet are:

- a laundry basket;
- a big picnic basket;
- a deep bureau or desk drawer;
- a plastic dairy foods delivery crate resting on a television frame on wheels.

Any of these items, naturally, has to be lined with soft padding of some kind. The whole theory behind the nest lined with padding and bumpers is not only to protect the newborn, but also to create a *small* space that will suggest the private, cozy, enclosed atmosphere of the womb, where the small one spent so many contented, secure months. Let your infant sleep away his first few months in the outside world in an oval wicker laundry basket suspended with stout ropes from the ceiling beam of your studio apartment. It's easy as pie

99

to rock him there, and the constant slight movement of this swinging cocoon will reproduce the feeling of being suspended in amniotic fluid.

As for the bathinette (or whatever its contemporary name is), the only reason I gave one house room when I had an infant son was that it was a gift from doting relatives whose feelings I couldn't hurt. My son soon graduated to bathing in the kitchen sink—a perfect "bathinette"—and was dressed or dried on any handy surface. (My granddaughter's progress was from a plastic stow-under-the-bed bathtub to the grownups' built-in tub, which she enjoyed as soon as she could sit.)

Let's assume you've now safely passed through the infancy stage without any major expenditure on furniture or decoration of your tiny flat and that you have moved into a two bedroom house, where Junior—now two or three years old—will have his own room, at last. It's a miniscule one, but still, it's all his own turf. The less expensive the "decoration" the better, for kids have a way of turning into teenagers before you can teach them "This Little Piggy Went to Market," and he will soon be doing his own refurbishing. Don't make the mistake, for example, of buying a crib or "youth bed" now; it's a waste of money. A studio-couch-size mattress-and-springs set is the ticket. Don't throw away good money by buying a bedstead in the form of a circus wagon or a space ship. (Yes, they are on the market, and the prices are astronomical!) Put the cash instead into a sturdy set of window bars if Junior's room is not street level (or, even if it is, and the neighborhood abounds in potential kidnappers), and keep him safe while imagining for himself that he is a circus monkey or a space man.

If a pleased aunt or grandparent has presented you with a beautiful wooden, iron, or brass crib, don't despair. When the baby has outgrown it, you can cut the legs down a bit, leave the side down permanently, cover the mattress with some decorator fabric, and use it for a chair or bench in the study, living room, or TV room.

It's a temptation, I know, to try to fill a small person's room with darling, antique small-sized furniture. Try to resist it. A standard-size chest of drawers, where he can use the drawers himself, from the bottom up, makes far more sense. It's a piece that grows with him. Baby-size chairs are cute and fun and can be pounded together in an afternoon by the handy home carpenter, using the four-piece principle of the sofa in Chapter 5. They can go out to the sun porch to hold plants later on. A baby scale, one of those old-style wicker ones, preferably, can be transferred later to the kitchen for holding fresh fruit and vegetables or to the living room for a plant holder.

Just in case you cut your eye teeth on that little chair just mentioned and want to go on to something more ambitious, what about building a bunk bed or study desk (combined table and chair)? Here is a desk you can make out of two pieces of 3/4-inch plywood, 21 by 25 inches.

How to Make a Little Person's Desk From Two Pieces of Plywood— Without a Jigsaw

Materials and Tools Needed:
two pieces 3/4-inch plywood, each 25 × 21 inches
drill and drill bits
curved-edge chisel
hammer
screwdriver
eighteen flat-headed screws, at least 1 1/2 inches long
pad saw
sandpaper
paint

Directions:
1. Mark one plywood board in the manner shown in the illustration. This will be one side plus the top of the desk.
2. Mark the other piece of plywood in the manner shown in the illustration. This will be the other side plus the chair seat, the chair back, and the brace board to hold the two sides together at the bottom.
3. With a bit wide enough in circumference to make a hole that will accommodate your pad saw, drill holes in the four corners marked "x," clear through the plywood.
4. Starting from these x marks, saw the inside rectangles out, rounding the chair-back corners when you come to them. You now have two picture-frame-like pieces of plyboard and two smaller rectangles.
5. Saw one of the 14- by 18-inch rectangles into pieces each 7 1/2, 3 1/2, and 3 inches wide. You now have all six pieces of your desk-and-chair set.
6. Measure 15 1/2 inches across the top of one picture frame; measure 3 1/2 inches in from the other side and draw lines at right angles, where the broken lines are in the illustration.

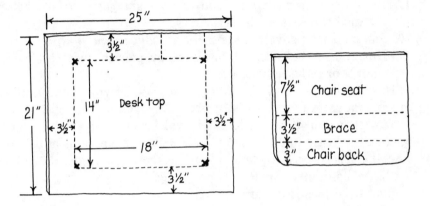

7. Using these lines to guide you, saw out a piece of wood 8 by 3 1/2 inches and put it into your scrap-wood bin.

8. Repeat steps 6 and 7 on the second picture frame. Now, except for rounding off the corners, all six pieces of your construction are ready to be assembled.

9. With the curved-edge chisel and a hammer, round off the seven outside corners of the two sides and the two front corners of the chair-seat board.

10. On one side board, mark drill holes in the manner shown in the illustration.

11. Repeat step 10 on second side board.

12. Change drill bit to one slightly smaller than your screws. Drill holes clear through the side boards at these eighteen locations marked "x."

13. Match desk top with the six holes along the tops of the side pieces. Using a thin pencil or pen, mark drill holes on both sides of desk top by inserting marker into holes.

14. Repeat step 13 with the brace board.

15. Repeat step 13 with the chair seat.

16. Repeat step 13 with the chair back.

17. Using the same drill bit, drill holes in these eighteen new locations to a depth of 3/4 inch.

18. Assemble desk by inserting screws into these eighteen locations and screwing the parts securely together.
19. Reinforce joinings with woodworker's glue, applied just before the final turnings of the screws.
20. Sandpaper all edges and corners to reduce their sharpness.
21. Now finish the piece of furniture by painting with high-gloss enamel or polyurethane paint.

This work table or desk-and-chair set will fit your child until he or she graduates to a flush-door-plus-filing-cabinet sort of desk.

Now that you've built a desk, it will be no problem for you to build a bookcase out of crate wood. Before it functions as a book-case, it can serve as a toy holder. Besides shelves, consider the following list of containers for Baby's playthings:

good-sized plastic laundry baskets;
orange crates (if you can find them);
heavy-duty cardboard boxes (such as the ones liquor stores have to throw away by the cartload);
rubberized wire dish drainers;
small nail kegs;
a series of laundry bags stitched out of pillow ticking or other sturdy cotton.

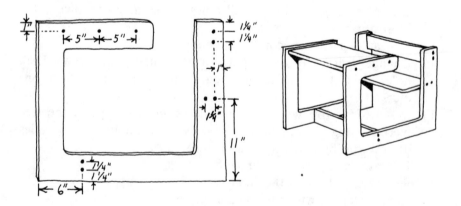

The simplest thing in the world is to build a floor chest or box of scrap wood and upholster it with a stout fabric, perhaps the faded material, reversed, that you've taken off that wing chair in the living room. If you add a hinged cover, be sure to upholster the lid, too, and your construction can now serve as seating. You will not only save some jammed fingers and splintered bottoms, but a container like this can move around your house later and fulfill a myriad of demands. I made one for my son's room out of scraps of wood picked up from Manhattan's sidewalks. Over the years it has held squishy toys, building blocks, electric train set, sports equipment, comic books in endless numbers, bedding, art supplies, and I forget what else. At present, it is used as a wood box near the fireplace. A box such as this might even become the muddy-boots box that stays by the front door.

If your little person's room boasts a clothes closet, chances are that the pole is too high for him to reach. Purchase a spring tension pole (or chinning bar) and attach it halfway down the closet walls. Now he can reach to hang up his clothes. Even a little trapeze suspended from the high bar is a good plan. Should you install a bar in more or less permanent form, don't worry: when the closet is used by an adult, the lower bar can hold all the "half" clothing such as shirts or blouses, jackets, short skirts, etc.

Speaking of closets, I once had friends who lived in a two-bedroom floor-through, where one narrow little room off the hall was allotted to their only son. (The room wasn't so much a bedroom as, I imagined when I saw it, an ex-linen closet.) The arrangement worked fine until son number-one was followed by number-two, then number-three, a year or so apart. With the arrival of number three son, they sent me an S.O.S. What to do? They *owned* the house and were paying off the mortage by renting out the more luxurious garden floor, so they couldn't just pick up and move. Happily, though the floor space in the boys' room was at a premium, the ceilings in that turn-of-the-century building were very high. My friends had sensibly installed a bunk bed to accommodate the boys when there were two, but some-how they couldn't imagine turning it into a three-decker. Which is— you've guessed it—precisely what I advised them to do. A plain ordi-nary house painter's wooden ladder with hooks attached to the top provided access to the middle and top bunks. The boys loved it, and drew lots for who slept where every few months. Fortunately, the room's one window was also a tall one, so that top man didn't have to sleep in a dark, airless little cul-de-sac.

Bunk-bed-like "environments" for children's rooms can be bought in any "swinging" furniture store, but the prices are high. If you have access to a reasonable lumber supply, why not have them cut the pieces of wood to your measurement and make a bunk bed yourself? In the city housing project where I once lived, my next-door neighbor did just that, thus solving her two-kids-in-one-small-bedroom problem. When she moved to the suburbs, she couldn't get the bunk bed out of the apartment. Guess who inherited the construction, lock, stock, and ladder? With just a little disassembling, I moved the whole thing (2 by 4 uprights, 1 by 4 horizontal frame pieces, plywood mattress bottoms) into my apartment, where it lived for years longer. By that time I'd acquired (on sale, of course) a full-size foam-rubber mattress-and-springs set for my son's room, so I erected only the top bunk over the double bed. It made a perfect landing site for small boys, who climbed the ladder and then took off like birds or airplanes from the top bunk. When these Superboys had grown into Supermen, we disassembled the structure once more and made the

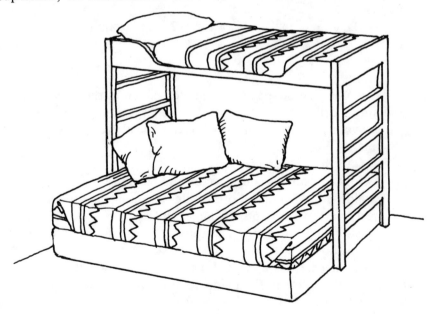

long, stout side boards into a narrow bookcase for a long corridor. The plywood top-bunk base was turned into a desk top (two metal two-drawer file cases, picked up cheap at an office furniture sale, provided the supports). Once you've got hold of some good solid wood, there are countless ways it can be used, combined with a little imagination. The ladder, if I remember correctly, went into the bathroom and served as a clothes dryer stretched across the bathtub.

Today, if I were going to build a bunk bed "environment" for a child's room, I would eliminate the ladder by constructing it out of six pieces of plywood with toe holes cut out of one end. Here's how to accommodate two kids in a too-small bedroom.

How to Build a Two-Child Bunk Bed

Materials and Tools Needed:
two plywood boards, each 1/2 × 75 × 32 1/2 inches (mattress supports)
two boards, each 3/4 × 66 × 76 1/2 inches (sides)
two boards, each 3/4 × 32 1/2 × 66 inches (head and foot)
eight 38-inch lengths of solid round steel curtain rod
sixteen knobs to fit the ends of the rods
drill, drill bit, and auger head
hammer
fifty-six flat-headed nails, at least 1 1/2 inches long
pad saw

Directions:
1. Mark one side board in the manner shown in the illustration. .
2. Using a drill bit that will bore a hole large enough to accommodate your pad saw, drill clear through the plywood at the two "x" spots.
3. Saw out the inner rectangle.
4. Saw out the curved-end piece on the bottom.
5. Two inches up from the bottom edge of the side board and spaced 2 feet apart, mark spots for augur holes.
6. Repeat step 5 on the top crosspiece of the side board for a total of eight holes.
7. Repeat steps 1 through 6 on the second side board.
8. Mark foot board in the manner shown in the illustration.
9. With the same drill bit you used in step 2, bore holes at eight spots marked "x," drilling clear through the plywood.

10. With pad saw, saw out these oval foot holes.
11. Saw out curved-end piece from bottom.
12. Mark headboard in the manner shown in the illustration.
13. Saw out curved-end piece from bottom.
14. Using augur head and the sixteen locations you marked in steps 5, 6, and 7, drill holes clear through the side boards.
15. Mark locations for thirty-two nails, eight on each end of the side boards, 3/8 inch in from the edges, evenly spaced.
16. Position foot- and headboards flush with ends of side boards;

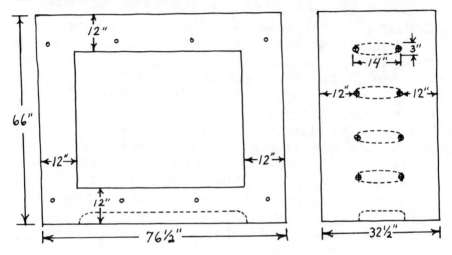

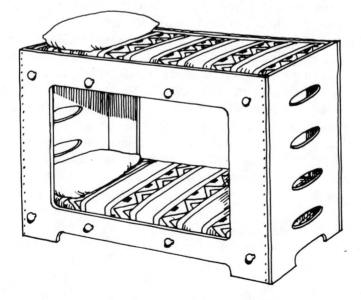

hammer nails through ends of side boards into edges of foot- and headboards.

17. Insert four steel rods through holes drilled for bottom bunk.
18. Place one mattress support board on steel rod support.
19. Hammer six nails through outside of headboard into head edge of mattress support board.
20. Hammer six nails through outside of footboard into foot edge of mattress support board.
21. Repeat steps 19 through 22, using the other eight rods and the mattress support board for the top bunk.
22. Push or screw knobs onto the protruding ends of the steel rods.

Now your two-bunk bed is completed; all you need to do is finish the wood in some way, by staining, painting, or oiling and waxing. Add mattresses and other bedding and you're in business. This simple construction is very robust and it will take a good deal of small-boy or -girl punishment. If you anticipate moving household soon, however, it might be better to substitute screws for the nails in this project. This will facilitate taking it apart to get it out of the house and into the moving van without ruining the finish on the wood parts.

If you cajoled the lumberyard to cut the parts for you, so that all you have to do is assemble the bunk bed, ask them to send the cutouts along with the parts. You can use them for table or desk tops, room dividers, or any number of small carpentry projects—if they don't charge you extra, naturally.

Most of the walls in a young child's room should be of a light, cheerful color of wood, washable paint, or easily cleanable wallpaper. Pegboard or corkboard panels on the walls of children's rooms are nifty, of course, because things can so easily be hung on them. Ditto for covering the walls with burlap, monk's cloth, or some such similar woven fabric. If there is one smallish, smooth wall in the room, consider covering it with blackboard paint. Apply it right on the wall, even if it's the door wall. Let the blackboard, without which no child should be, constitute the wall itself, including the door if it's, for example, a metal flush door. Keep chalk and eraser in a small plastic bucket (the one that's sprung a crack so is no longer waterworthy) near this wall. This effect, besides being smart designing and a great space-saver, may save you from scrubbing off watercolor paints from the less accommodating walls in your home.

Windows in a child's room offer an opportunity for whimsy that would be out of place in the formality of the living room. Once you have made them secure against accidents, study Baby's windows with an eye to playfulness; and cleanliness. In the sooty city a clever way to treat an infant's windows is to tack (or staple) cheesecloth (dyed pastel shades if you wish) right over the entire window frame. Two thicknesses will keep a lot of dirt-laden air out of your child's lungs while letting sufficient light through. Cheesecloth is cheap enough for you to simply take these "curtains" down every few months and discard them, grit and all. If fresh, unpolluted air outside the window is your bounty, then you may want to consider curtaining Baby's window in one of the following ways:

Dacron batiste (no-iron) ruffled Cape Cods;

three-tiered cafe curtains in a washable part-cotton floral or animal print;

bath towels or sheets in suitable colors or prints;

flannelette "receiving blankets" sewn together (which Baby, of course, has outgrown);

colored tissue paper glued right onto the window panes in free-form designs;

straight-falling curtains in shower-curtain-like plastic;

window shades onto which have been pasted cutouts (of sun, moon, stars, or other easy shapes) of adhesive-backed tape;

striped awnings stretched over a wooden (or metal) frame.

Before he begins to walk, and perhaps for a while afterwards, the baby's room is where you should keep that rocking chair that just doesn't seem to fit into any other room in the house. Then when he has been rocked back to sleep at night you don't have too far to carry him. Great wooden rocking chairs can often be picked up at country auctions for pennies, simply because they have lost a couple of spokes or slats from their backs—a cinch to replace. Other chairs for an older child's room are "made" by compiling stacks of pillows.

A chair that hangs from the ceiling or a beam can make all the difference in a child's room; or a simple wooden-seated swing suspended from the door frame. Just be sure the construction of your house or apartment can support this sort of punishing weight and activity and that there's room for the arc made by the moving swing. If so, there's probably nothing that will make a city kid more popular with his peers than having his own indoor swing!

Other things that should hang in a child's room are homemade mobiles. A plastic "Snow White and the Seven Dwarves" in a clamp-on commercially produced mobile, dancing in the air over the infant's crib, is all very nice, but you can exercise your creative bent so well with a more imaginative set of danglers cut out of cardboard and tied with various lengths of string to a metal coat hanger. Or here's another idea.

How to Make a Mobile From Things Found in the Kitchen Drawer

Materials and Tools Needed:
a one-bar, screw-into-the-wall towel rack
screwdriver and screws
metal-and-paper bag-end twists, thin wire, or string
cardboard
metal foil
scissors

Directions:
1. Mark holes in the window or door frame where screws will go and start the screw holes with a nail.
2. Screw towel rack into wall.
3. Cut fruit shapes out of the cardboard, such as an apple, banana, pear, grapes, eggplant, or any other shapes you like.
4. Wrap each piece of fruit in tin foil, some flat and some used, and thus scrunched into a textural contrast with the pristine metal.
5. Punch a hole through each piece and thread it with string, wire, or metal twists.
6. Suspend each piece from the towel rack or from another piece of fruit.

The metal twists will not make as mobile a mobile as the string or thin wire, but this will be a way of making some good use of that drawerful of little objects you've taken off packages of bread, cookies, etc., for which you never thought you'd ever create a utilitarian second life!

Most of the decorating of a child's room, as soon as he is of school age, should be left to the child himself, and he should be encouraged to let his lair reflect his own personality and talents. Children's school or after-school artwork, plus a roll of sticky tape, solves the wallcovering problem nicely. Natural objects that kids like to collect, such as shells, stones, leaves, feathers, butterflies, and moths, can make interesting decoration. Even some that are not so "natural" can also function as furbishment in a child's room if you can persuade yourself not to be uptight about What Art Is. Is your child, like countless others when in the serious collecting phase, ga-ga over bottle caps? At first you think, how ghastly. Then try working with him in making bas-relief designs of them on stiff cardboard. Painted white and mounted on a black background, even metal bottle caps take on an austere beauty. So would vari-sized and vari-colored plastic caps and spray-can tops in a similar setting.

If your child has a thing about match folders or is mad for aluminum pop-tops, don't discourage him. See that the dangerous elements are removed and then let the child string them up on long ribbons or string and festoon walls or air space with them. What harm can it do?

Should your child become an avid collector of ice-cream-pop sticks, encourage him to "tidy up the river banks." He can then make displays of them by pasting them onto cardboard or construction paper. Even a collection of burned wooden kitchen matches can be turned into a handsome wall hanging when pasted onto a cardboard or wood background in free- or not-so-free design. If you think these notions are not very classy, I can tell you that an art school in New York City once awarded first prize in a contest they ran for students and other adults in the neighborhood to a lovely, swirly "painting" made of burned wooden matches!

The masks the children made from papier mâché or bought at the five-and-dime store for Halloween make good wall decorations on November first. So do the faces carved in coconut shells that they made at summer camp or the Yuletide wreaths they put together at 4-H or Scout meetings. Finger paintings, magazine collages, or the first attempts at macramé, weaving, or needlepoint make fine decoration. Just try not to feel that a "Smokey the Bear" calendar for a boy's room or a Degas print of ballet dancers for a girl's are the only possible wall hangings.

Young children, since they're so urgently involved in the process, are fascinated with growth, particularly their own. Do you remember the pencil marks on the back of the closet door that showed how tall you were on your fifth, sixth, seventh birthdays? Why not institution-alize this practice and decorate a door or wall in your growing child's room? Glue a tape measure on the door or paint a facsimile yardstick on one wall? Or, put up a felt giraffe or quilted cotton ostrich with measurements running up its exaggerated neck?

If the floorboards of a child's room aren't all they should be, it's best to lay down some rubber-backed linoleum. That material takes far better to hurled juice bottles, modeling clay, and finger paints than wood, anyway, and you eliminate the possibility of splinters in small bottoms, knees, and fingers. When childhood is over, and you want to lay a good hardwood floor, the linoleum can have a second life on the floors of closets, mud rooms, or entryways. Now you can add a braided rag rug. For notes on rug-making, see Chapters 6 and 10.

Rags, if they're not used up in rugs, can stuff outsize toys made of fabric. Try your hand at multiplying the pattern for that stuffed sea horse, pussy cat, automobile, or train engine that you made in min-iature for a new-baby gift and then stuffing it very stiff with rags and other leftovers to make a piece of "furniture" or object for rough-and-tumble play. Sat on, lounged upon, pummeled and kicked and shoved around, these items can save a lot of wear-and-tear on "proper" furni-ture. Many mail-order catalogs carry these stuffed monsters, but building one yourself is cheaper and a lot more satisfying than send-ing for one. And it can become a conversation piece in the family room when the young person has tired of it in his own room.

Possibly the very best piece of furniture you can add to a small child's room isn't furniture at all, but the carton that some stove, breakfront, or television set came in. Look for a huge carton in the corridor of the apartment building where you live. Or watch your next-door neighbors' deliveries carefully and beg from her the carton her new wing chair came in. Bring it into your house, cut windows and a door in it. Tell your child something like "I wish this were a tree house, but perhaps this will do," and watch the eyes light up. The youngster and several pals will have months and months of pleasure from this ad hoc playhouse, at a cost of not one penny. It allows the imagination free rein, like some of the very best manufactured chil-dren's toys and like some of the very best decorating schemes.

TIPS

- *If you have furnished an infant's room with some unpainted wooden furniture and are tempted to wax or linseed-oil it— don't! These substances may find their way into Baby's digestive system, which will not benefit by them. An application of some light, edible vegetable oil, however, can do no harm.*
- *A short person reaching up to a wooden clothes-hanging rod will have trouble sliding the hangers along it, unless the pole is treated from time to time with a light coating of paste wax.*
- *Children's parties often provide leftovers that can become decorations for little people's rooms. For example, after the youngsters have played "Pin the Tail on the Donkey," why not install the several-tailed beast as a permanent wall hanging?*
- *In a school-age child's room with no space for a desk, a wooden student chair with an arm-rest writing surface is useful. Such a chair can also be a decorative asset if enameled the wall color or covered with the same cotton fabric as the drapes or bedspread. Simply smooth the cotton, cut into pieces that fit the chair parts, over an application of white glue.*

6

Room for Working, Playing, and Other Aspects of Living

The sitting room has become, in the last decade or so, something called the "conversation pit"; what we used to know as the living room has devolved in most contemporary houses to the "family room"; and anyone alluding to the parlor is regarded as an antediluvian relic. Ergo, this rather roundabout chapter title for the space that is usually the largest in an apartment of more than two rooms, the room in a house that customarily commands the most urgent attention from the home decorator. In European countries, it may be called the "reception room" or the "salon." Whatever its name, this is the room that establishes the whole tone of your home life. It reflects most immediately to the outside world what you are and do; thus, it merits all the imagination and ingenuity you can summon up in thinking about its design.

The most rigid of interior designers will insist that your living room must have a focal point—one point toward which the eye is irresistibly drawn upon entrance to the room. The best of interior decorators realizes that in a room of any size at all there will be not one, but several, focal points, *each* of which should be something good to look at. This doesn't preclude the object's functionality; nor does it mean it has to cost a lot of money, or any money at all. One focal point can be part of the room's architecture, such as a fireplace or a window. Another may be the beautiful Chinese rug you inherited on the floor, on the wall, or even draped over the railing of the stairway that rises out of the room, or the wool-rag rug you braided yourself. That particularly handsome lamp you put together with assorted parts from kitchen and hardware store provides a focal point when it throws light in interesting patterns against wall or ceiling (see pages 131 to 136 for some good lamps to make). An inviting sofa is certainly a focal point for a living room, and so is a beautiful batik wall hanging, or even an elegantly framed gravestone rubbing you made on your visit to New England.

You've heard a lot about "balancing" a room else it will look unpleasantly lopsided; there is something in this. If all your heavy pieces are bunched together on one side of the room, your guests may get a feeling of seasickness from your decor. In a medium-size room color needs to be balanced, too. In fact, color can abet the illusion of balance where it doesn't exist. Furniture that is lighter in color tone will appear lighter in bulk and weight than it actually is; whereas a solid, bold blue or red slipcover on a chair may not only balance your color scheme, but camouflage the fact that a spindly chair is occupying the space that obviously calls for more weight and solidity. In fact, your heaviest piece of furniture should not be against a wall, if you can manage it, but in the central part of the room. But, if this is not feasible, then perhaps a pistachio-colored slipcover or a coat of white paint will make it look a bit less ponderous.

The amateur decorator is usually able to work this principle of balance into his furniture arrangement and still make sensible placements that don't block access (or egress), cut off natural light, or make it impossible for more than one person to have a sitting conversation. But one thing the budget designer sometimes overlooks is the boring condition that exists in a living room where almost everything in the room is the same height, at one level. Though this may make perfect sense for the human adult body, it is tedious for the eye. Running a shelving unit up to the ceiling helps, as does the presence of one very high-backed chair, such as a peacock chair—one of those fanback wicker ones—a high wing-chair, or a Spanish or Italian carved wooden chair. Adding to the room one very tall plant, such as a rubber or other variety of Ficus will break the monotony, as will a dried arrangement of lengthy weeds and grasses. Pampas grass, a tall strawlike reed with a feathery top, can be gathered from swampy regions and put in an umbrella stand with a sprinkling of peacock feathers for a stunning decorative effect that also lends height to your room.

If, when you look around your principal room, you see that bookcases, dining table, desk top, chair backs, sofa back, and everything else stop at the same distance from the floor, you can break it up by hanging an attractive belt (perhaps of Mexican woven tapestry or

Israeli silk) from the ceiling near one corner of the room. Or, train a pot of ivy to climb up a little homemade lattice placed behind the flowerpot on the bookshelf top. A tall, slender wooden sculpture could do it, or a butterfly collection behind Lucite, arranged as if flying in formation up to the ceiling. Even a fern in a hanging pot would do the trick. Anything goes, just as long as there is something to draw the eye away from that waist-high level at which so many furnishings stop growing.

The "givens" in most living rooms are ceilings, walls, floors, doors, and windows. It's what you do with them that counts. Let's imagine a living room devoid of furniture and see where we should start. Perhaps at the top. The best thing to do with a ceiling you've not yet lived under is to paint it a light color if it's a low room, somewhat darker if it's a high room. In fact, if moving into a living room that bears the cobwebs and sticky-finger marks of a previous occupant, you can't go very wrong by painting the whole room, walls and ceiling, the same neutral shade. A whitewash job all over is what a decorator friend of mine always does to a living room she's been asked to "do," so she "can see where she's at." If the window-and-door trim needs attention, include those surfaces too in your painting. Later, you can decide whether you want wallpaper or fabric for wall and ceiling covering, and if that ebony or deep purple is really the color that should frame doors and windows. If your background paint is a light neutral color, such as bone or beige, you'll save money when you redecorate by needing only one coat to cover it.

If you are undecided as to whether you'll carpet wall-to-wall or lay a new hardwood floor over an old scarred pine underpinning, the most efficacious thing to do with the floor is to paint it over, not, this time, with a light, neutral but with a dark brown or black enamel. This will give you time to think out how you want to treat your floor, to discover whether you need rugs for insulation or decoration, or whether the parquet or vinyl tiles you put down should be left uncovered.

While you're contemplating saving up for a big, splashy purchase of broadloom, or a flokati or rya area rug, or thinking about investing in rug-hooking equipment, why not make a temporary braided rug for the living room floor? A bagful of cotton rags can turn into a useful braided rug. Or, for a more durable and handsome rug, use old, woolen skirts, jackets, and suits that are no longer wearable.

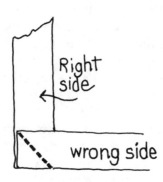

Just cut the fabric into strips, 2 inches wide, and sew them together into three lengths of equal measurement. The secret—and about the only real trick in rug-braiding—is to stitch the lengths of fabric together on the bias, in the manner described in the illustration.

Tack the three long strips to a board and simply braid them, turning the cut edges of material under as you proceed, flattening the braid at the same time. Now coil the braid into a flat round or oval shape and sew the edges of the braid together as you do so. The size rug you can make this easy way is limited only by the amount of fabric you have collected—and your patience. It's best to work with lengths no more than 4 feet long, else the tangling of the unbraided ends may involve you in a messy situation. As soon as you get to the end of the first three strands, hand sew the next three to them, and so on. All one color is nice, but a variegated rug is good, too. And though it blends very well with traditional furniture, this kind of rug goes equally well with more streamlined fittings.

You can achieve a higher-nap rug by cutting the lengths somewhat wide, stitching them together into long tubes, and stuffing the tubes with cotton, nylon, foam rubber crumbs, or fabric scraps of the same stuff as the tubes. I personally don't like the look of braided rugs made this way, but you may.

A word or two about color in the living room. If the room isn't absolutely baronial, it will be best to stick to no more than two basic colors for wide expanses or large objects; and they ought to come from opposite sides of the color spectrum, that is, "complementary" colors. Examples are red and green, blue and orange, purple and yellow, or versions of these. Accents can be in third and fourth color ranges. This excludes white, black, and brown, which aren't colors at all in the sense we're now speaking. A good way to tie a house or apartment together, giving it decorative coherence, is to carry accent shades through the door into the next room, where they can become the basic colors for the new room.

If your desire for a custom-made overstuffed divan in front of the fireplace has never been realized, don't despair. With eight cushions, a little lumber, and a handful of hardware, you can come up with a dramatic sofa that would cost you in the neighborhood of 500 dollars custom-made. Here's how even the not-terribly-handy carpenter can get a fine new sofa.

How to Build Your Own Sofa

Materials and Tools Needed:
two solid 3/4-inch planks, each 72 × 24 inches (seat and back)
two solid 3/4-inch planks, each 36 × 36 inches (sides)
rasp file
sandpaper
hammer and chisel
drill and drill bits
screws
woodworker's glue

Directions:
1. As soon as the lumberyard delivers them, "polish" the wood planks to a velvety finish: sand the whole surface and file the corners and edges to a good roundness (except the edges of the long boards that will be joined to each other or be sunk into the side boards).
2. Determine what will be the inside of one of the side boards, and, on this surface, measure in 1 inch from the top back corner and make a mark.
3. Still working on the inside of the same board, measure 26 inches

down the back edge and then in toward the center 6 inches. Make another mark.

4. Connect these two marks with a straight line.
5. Draw a line parallel to the first line, 7/8 inch away and toward the center of the board.
6. At right angle to the lower end of the first line, draw a straight line of 26 inches toward the front edge of the board.
7. Draw a line parallel to the one in step 6, 7/8 inch from it. These four lines outline the grooves you will cut.
8. Determine what will be the inside of the second side board; on its surface repeat steps 2 through 7.
9. With chisel and hammer, cut grooves about 1/4-inch deep in both side boards.
10. Apply glue to the edges of the plank that will become the sofa seat and to the groove that will receive it in both side boards.
11. With one side of the sofa against the wall and a heavy piece of furniture against the other side, allow the glue to harden over-night.
12. Apply glue to the straight (unsanded) long edge of the other (back) board and to the grooves in the side boards that will re-ceive it.
13. Slide the back board into place and allow the glue to harden.
14. For reinforcement, drill a few holes through side boards into the edges of seat and back boards and apply screws (or bolts). A total of eight should suffice.

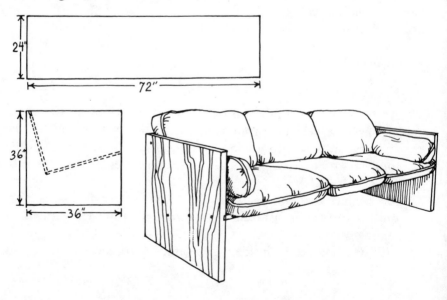

15. Now is the time (if you wish to do it) to finish the wood by stain-
    ing, oiling, waxing, or a combination of these.
16. Position the cushions and you're all set.

A less formal kind of a divan can be made for a "loungey" kind
of a room with upholstery or slip-covering fabric. Sew up a tube of
fabric, 20 feet long and 30 inches around. Stuff it with rags, cotton/
nylon stuffing, or bits of foam rubber from that mattress that is about
to be replaced. Twist this long cylinder into a pretzel shape or a loose
square knot. And, voilà! You have a sofa that (hold your hat) sells
for nearly 300 dollars in some department stores!

Seating is a sine qua non of the living room; but where is it written
that two matching armchairs and a sofa are the only possible seating
surfaces? I was about to say "look at the conversation pit" when I
remembered how much I detest that particular bit of split-level contemporary nonsense. As if you had to build a little arena lined with
benches before the people gathered in a room could begin to talk
with one another! The conversation pit does, however, illustrate the
point that sitting needn't take place only on the rigid combination
of sofa and two chairs. Seating that you can make yourself easily
without a visit to the lumberyard can be fashioned from four sofa
pillows and three zippers. You don't even need a sewing machine; in
fact, it's preferable to construct this piece of furniture by hand
sewing.

How to Make a Comfortable Chair by Hand

Materials and Tools Needed:
four equal-size rectangular sofa pillows of the non-square-cornered
    kind
enough sturdy cotton fabric to cover all four pillows
two zippers, as long as the width of the pillows
one zipper, twice the length of the pillows
needle and thread

Directions:
1. Make the cover for the first pillow by laying the pillow on the fabric
   to measure how much and then sewing it up, making stitches right

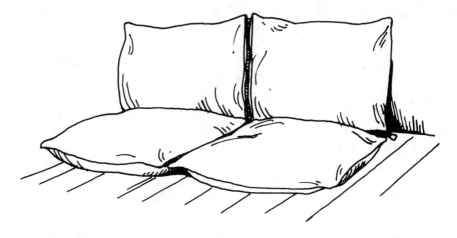

into the pillow if you want. Or, stitch up three sides with fabric inside out and then stuff it and sew the last side right side out.

2. Repeat step 1 with the other three pillows.

3. Using one of the smaller zippers, sew one side of the zipper to one shorter edge of one of the pillows and the other side of the zipper to the shorter edge of another of the pillows.

4. Repeat step 3 with the other smaller zipper and the other two pillows. Now you have the back and the seat of the chair completed. Close up the zippers.

5. To put the two sections together, sew one side of the longer zipper along the long edge of one of the two-pillow units; sew the other side of the longer zipper along the long edge of the other two-pillow unit. Close the zipper fastening. Your chair is all ready to be leaned against a wall or the back of a heavy bookcase or other piece of freestanding furniture.

This chair can cost about 200 dollars in a department store. If you've picked up the pillows from the sidewalk, the fabric at a Tag Sale, and one of the zippers out of an old housecoat you've hardly worn, that's about 198 dollars saved.

Toney furniture establishments also advertise something called a Lofa, "A very new and very smart idea in furniture," which looks from its pictures like nothing so much as the chair above, in a larger size but at a lower cost: 159 dollars. The difference may be that it's filled with air or even water, though it looks to be stuffed with foam rubber. It makes for very comfortable seating for today's informal living, and you can make it a lot cheaper, its beauty dependent only on your own innate good taste in picking out fabrics.

You can't go wrong in the selection of fabrics if you remember one rule that *is* worth paying attention to: in a small- or medium-sized room, or in one area of a divided room, it's best to avoid too many busily patterned fabrics on wall, drapes, furniture, floors. A solid color can work well as accompaniment with one figured pattern plus one stripe or geometric pattern without creating nervousness or an uneasy atmosphere.

The elegance you can achieve in your home decorating with really good fabric is limitless. So it may pay you to go all out for a really distinguished piece of fabric once in a while, even if you have to pay for it. Even the decorating departments of high-falutin shops occasionally get stuck with what seems like an unsaleable amount (the end of a roll) of a beautiful silk, cotton, or polyester-mix and let it go at a ridiculous price. And, of course, if you live near one, you know that the mill-end remnant shop is a gold mine for the economy decorator. Invest in one of these finds once in a while, even if you don't see an immediate use for the remnant. Sooner or later, you'll come into possession of a broken-down old chair you'll want to repair and slip-cover with that stashed-away material, whereupon the chair will have a whole new life.

Now that we've got two- or three-seaters out of the way, let's talk more about chairs. An armchair or two certainly does belong in the living room, of all rooms; but again, you don't have to have a matched pair of Chippendale chairs with tufted backs and mahogany arms or even one of the Louis'. The long sofa on one side of the fireplace, facing the twin armchairs across a centered coffee table, is so standard an arrangement that it's sort of boring. Why not this: the sofa facing the fireplace, a wooden rocking chair to one side of it, and on the other side a couple of unmatching armchairs? Or, the sofa going across the room at an angle, a group of ottomans placed around the room here and there, and one armchair in one corner? Put one of the ottomans in front of the armchair and you'll never need one of those monstrosities with a crank on one side that tilt their backs down and their fronts up to form a stretch-out footrest. Really, a home-made footstool plus an armchair (whether homemade or from your transferred neighbor's garage sale) is so much more attractive and comfortable. Put the Barcalounger or its relative out onto the patio.

Don't give it precious houseroom! Armchair and stool don't have to "match" in furniture style; you can give them coherence by using the same fabric on chair and stool cushion.

The butterfly chair seems to have had its day. Perhaps the unsuspecting American public, on whom it was foisted, has finally realized that the resulting curvature of the spine wasn't worth the advantage of buying one frame that lasts forever and all you have to do is make yourself a new seat of canvas every couple of years. Its cousin, the director's chair, in all its manifestations, goes on forever; still comfortable, durable, inexpensive, compatible with any style or period of furniture. Since the director's chair folds up with such facility and is so easy to give a face-lift to, I don't know why anyone ever discards one. But I'm awfully glad they do because I have two, inherited years ago from a redecorating friend. They have been dressed in every color of the rainbow in duck or canvas seats and backs I've made for them. These two have lived useful decorative lives in four-going-on-five living rooms. I wouldn't dream of moving household without them. Right now—one in somber black and the other in cool turquoise—they are the TV-watching seats, pressed into service for dining when there is company. I don't see how any economically decorated home can possibly do without a couple of director's chairs. If you're all thumbs and don't want to try making the replacement seats and backs, buy them at a discount house when you feel like changing the living room color scheme.

If new coverings for seating is indicated and you've just used up your budget allotment on the director's chairs, you may be able to get away with keeping the fabric on the love seat a bit longer, despite the ineradicable spot that lies smack in the middle of the backrest. (Probably some guest wasn't too dextrous with the canapés at your cocktail party last week.) If you have no matching material leftover from the flea market fabric with which you upholstered the love seat, why not simply go through the closet to see if you can find a lovely shawl, stole, or scarf that can be casually draped over the blemish? Another trick for postponing reupholstering when a couple of cigarette holes, for instance, have appeared in the seat is to cover the hole or holes diagonally with an ambassadorial stripe of contrasting fabric across sofa back and seat.

Don't quake at the sound of that word "upholster," by the way. Upholstering doesn't necessarily mean calling in a professional at huge expense. If you're not spooked by the term itself, you won't bog down in the process. All it means is to apply a permanent fabric covering to a piece of furniture. First you remove the tacks and/or stitching and then the upholstery fabric. Now you have in hand a ready-made pattern for cutting out the new fabric. Simply retack and/or restitch the new fabric onto the chair or divan, fastening it at the same spots where the old fabric was attached.

If you decide to leave the old fabric on and upholster over it, cut a pattern from an old sheet or some such remnant in your rag bag. Trim it to shape by placing it on the furniture part it is to cover. It's always best not to plunge right into the costly fabric itself with your scissors. Judging the size and shape of the part by eye alone is dangerous. But with either of these simple methods, even "Old Butterfingers" can have brilliant success with the first foray into upholstering.

Slipcovering chairs and divans should not be a bugaboo to the economical home decorator either. So much a product of the Machine Age was I when I first embarked on slipcovering that I felt the fact that my ancient rebuilt Singer was temporarily out of service should exempt me from trying. But fingers were made before Singers (or Necchis or Brothers), and there's no reason why you can't hand-stitch a slipcover. In fact, if you're putting welting into the seams, machinelessness may be an advantage. If your machine lacks a welting foot, you're really better off working those thick seams by hand.

On the subject of tables, entire books can be and have been written. I will try to restrict the subject to a few pages. It's difficult, though, because the table—and in this case I'm talking about the occasional table, not the workaday, sturdy dining table cum worktable cum desk top—is one of my favorite pieces of furniture. It's so easy to make out of nothing. Found objects plus a little imagination are responsible for a stunning array of costless tables. In any garage, barn, or backyard are at least a hundred things that can become table bottoms; in kitchen, bedroom, or attic tabletops abound. For handsome and useful coffee tables and end tables it's simply a matter of putting them together.

Let's play a game. I've listed in the left-hand column all sorts of natural table bases, and in the right-hand column, found-object tops. All you need do is match them, one object from the right side placed on top of one from the left. See what kicky combinations you can work out.

Table Bases

Nail keg
Hatbox
Tree stump section
Telephone pole section
Garbage pail
Water or milk pail
Pickling crock
Egg basket
Hat rack bottom
Luggage rack
Bricks
Cinder blocks
Galvanized metal tub
Canning kettle
Large flowerpot
Flour firkin
Sand-filled coffee cans
Picnic hamper or other basket
Footstool
Drum
Cork squares pile
Bureau or desk drawers on end
Drain or flue tiles
Flat-topped stone
Metal pedestal from wrecking yard
Wrought-iron legs from five-and-dime store
Upended mailbox

Tabletops

Cabinet door
Retired bulletin board
Marble slab
Piece of slate
Plate glass or Lucite
Mirror in an ornate picture frame
Breadboard
Piano stool top
Piano bench top
Serving tray
Child's board game

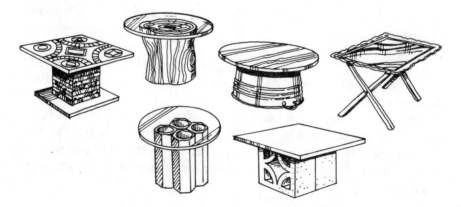

You can clearly see that the right-hand column was beginning to wear thin, whereas the left-hand could have gone on forever. That's partly because so many of the left-hand items make good little coffee or end tables in and of themselves, while the right-hands are simply flat surfaces, which you can recognize without any help from me. If you have in your living room a "made-up" table that is not a version of one of these combinations, please write and tell me about it.

Don't tell me that its base is a steamer trunk. Little old trunks (with or without something flat laid on top) are often used for end tables or coffee tables. For the latter, they have always struck me as being most awkward, as have the solid cubes that decorators contemporarily set such great store by. A butcher block cube may be had for around 20 dollars, while a glass one can cost 50 dollars and up. My objection to this sort of coffee table is that it doesn't seem to go with the natural position of the sitting human body. Since you can't slide your feet under it, such a table seems an unnatural item to set drinks on and sip or eat from.

If you don't share this objection, an item you may want to pick up at an auction or from a printer going out of business is a type cabinet. The old ones of oak or walnut are quite impressive looking and make good block-type coffee tables. If you live in a loft, a converted barn, or other informal situation with a large living room, try to capture from the street, highway, or a building site one of those much-desired cable spools. If a cable spool is not something you chance upon every day, why not make yourself one by joining two circles of wood with a round or square column of wood? It's a very simple coffee table to make.

A really peachy coffee table can be acquired by certain winter sports fans for nothing. If you can't think where to store your toboggan for the summer months, it's easy: turn it upside down in front of the divan on two sections of tree trunk. The curved-over portion in the front, now underneath, becomes a good magazine rack. I suppose that when the tobogganing season is on, you can press your water skis into service in the same way!

The Parsons School of Design in New York City gathers some of the best furniture-design minds in the United States today. Their perfectly simple, unadorned, flat-topped, four-legged, rectangular or round tables that fit any situation you can think of are an example of excellent design, in which less is more. These tables, constructed of wood, metal, glass, plastic, or some combination of these materials, are very expensive. However, so obvious and clean-lined is the design that copies of them started to be marketed immediately after the line was launched by Parsons. You can now buy a smallish, white plastic end table in cut-rate chain stores for little more than 3 dollars. It's a fabulous buy in good design.

If you have been given a table and you like all of the proportions except for its height, what could be simpler? Cut the legs down until it's coffee-table (or whatever) distance from the floor. And, if you like everything about your coffee table except its non-stainproof top, why not cover it with some material that *will* take cups and glasses without making rings? Tiles left over from doing your bathroom, for example, will work. If you don't have enough tiles to cover the entire tabletop, lay the tile around the edges, where cups or glasses will be set down, and fill in the middle with a new piece of wood, or make a border of flattened-out tin or aluminum cans. Make them nice and smooth by rolling them with a lawn roller and glue them to the border of the tabletop, or nail them on with decorative upholstery tacks.

So much for tables. If you still want to buy one new, at least don't pay full list retail price for it. Get it from a seasonal or warehouse-clearing sale, or find it marked down because it has lived a life of hard knocks in a department store. "As is" prices are surprisingly small fractions of the original prices, and this "condition" usually means there is some very small defect or marring that you can hide or correct with ease.

In the room where you do most of your working and playing, you surely need some lamps. Even if the ceiling unit is sufficient for transforming midnight into noon, a floor lamp for the reading chair plus a table lamp for "decor" may not be amiss. Make yourself a couple and enjoy a terrific sense of achievement. With a little help from your friends at the hardware store, you can save lots of dollars this way. The things that can be turned into lamp bases are legion, of course. Since you hardly need be told about wicker-covered wine bottles and stoneware molasses jugs and the like, I'm going to limit myself to one each of four general categories of lamps you can make.

Before I do, however, let me put in a word for the good, standard, efficient desk lamp that you may think looks too "officey" for use in a home. You know, one of those jobs on the end of a movable metal arm, with the solid metal base, the gooseneck lamp and its more modern relatives that take neon tubes for bulbs. There really is nothing much superior for reading in bed, working at a desk, or reading in a chair, and a coat of paint in a bedroom or parlor color will do wonders for blending such a lamp into your decoration. Some of the metal-shaded ones can even be fitted out with fabric (that matches something in the room) and glued to the metal shade. That treatment does a lot to "de-office" such a lamp.

Here, now, are a bevy of beautiful lamps to light up your living room without lightening your pocketbook by much.

How to Make a Streamlined Floor Lamp

Materials and Tools Needed:
5 feet of 4-inch-wide white plastic drainpipe
one white plastic drainpipe elbow joint
one round porcelain lamp socket and seating, 4 inches in diameter
one round plastic dairy-foods container, with 4 1/2-inch top diameter
three hefty bricks
an old belt
plastic glue
putty
saw
an outsize frosted round light bulb

Directions:
1. Fit the elbow joint onto one end of the plastic drainpipe.
2. Saw a small notch in the other end of the plastic drainpipe.
3. Apply glue around the end of the underside of the porcelain seating and press it against the ridge inside the elbow joint, making sure the electrical cord is going down through the drainpipe.
4. Cut a hole in the bottom of the dairy-foods container and fix it to the porcelain seating with a snake of putty.
5. Apply another snake of putty to the circle where the porcelain seating meets the plastic elbow joint.
6. Put the three bricks together in a triangle and hold them in place with the belt.
7. Pull the electric cord out through the notch in the drainpipe and insert the drainpipe into the brick base.

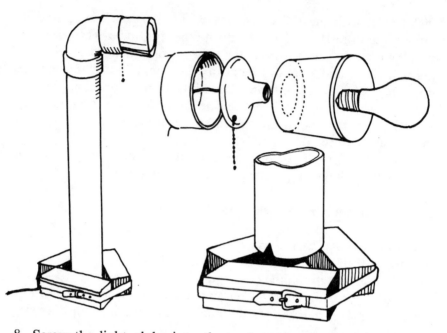

8. Screw the light globe into the socket, plug the cord into a wall plate—and you're in business.

This same sort of lamp could be made from one of those stout cardboard tubes often used to hold carpeting sold by the yard. In that case, you'd probably want to paint, wrap with fabric, or wallpaper the tube. The white plastic drainpipe, on the other hand, has a very smart contemporary look.

How to Make an Inexpensive Table Lamp

Materials and Tools Needed:

three terra-cotta flowerpots, 8 1/2 inches in top diameter (the lip-less pots make a smoother-lined lamp, but the lipped ones can be used, too)

one light socket with on-off button on side and cord coming out the bottom

1 square foot of 3/8- or 3/4-inch plywood

one light bulb

woodworker's glue

putty

saw (or chisel)

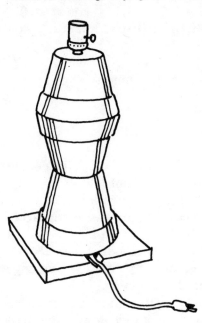

Directions:

1. Cut or chisel a groove in the plywood from its center to the middle of one side.
2. Pile the flowerpots up, end to end, with top and bottom ones upside down and middle one right side up.
3. Glue the flowerpots together in this position, allowing the glue to harden for several hours.
4. Screw the lamp socket into the drainage hole in the top pot, allowing the cord to extend downwards.
5. Fix the socket to the top pot with a snake of putty.
6. Positioning the cord in the groove in the plywood, glue the bottom edge of the bottom flowerpot to the plywood base and allow the glue to harden.
7. Add the light bulb and the lamp is finished, unless you don't fancy the terra-cotta and plywood finish, in which case you can paint the whole thing your favorite colors.

How to Make a "Sculptured" Hanging Lamp

Materials and Tools Needed:
a cord and socket hanging from the ceiling (the "given" in this case)
a large funnel, 8 to 10 inches across pouring top

a 2-foot yard of light-colored stretch fabric (nylon or cotton jersey,
   for example)
needle and thread
narrow-gauge copper or aluminum tubing
picture-hanging wire
saw

Directions:
1. Cut the small end of the funnel off at the point where its diameter
   will fit onto the socket and not fall off.
2. Sew the long sides of the stretch fabric together into a tube.
3. From the tubing cut four or five sections of equal or varying
   lengths.
4. Cut wire in lengths 2 inches longer than each section of tubing.
5. Make hoops of the tubing sections by running wire through and
   twisting it together for a joining.
6. Secure one end of the stretch-fabric tube to the wide end of the
   funnel, which is hanging upside down from the ceiling on the cord
   and socket.
7. Push the metal hoops into the tube of fabric at intervals.

8. Sew the bottom hoop into place at the bottom of the fabric tube; the other hoops will be held in place by the stretchiness of the fabric.

The white nylon jersey (or whatever stretch fabric) will curve in between the tubing circles in a graceful, pleasing manner, reminiscent of a marble column. Its length and convolutions will be limited only by your patience in fashioning the circular tubes of light metal. Your patience will not be tried at all if you should find in the village dump a group of firkin hoops, or even old lampshade frame circles, that will fill the bill for the ribbing.

How to Make a Colander Globe Lamp

Materials and Tools Needed:
two three-legged metal colanders
a lamp socket in a porcelain seating
a light bulb
a 4-foot lamp cord with on-off button halfway along it
paper clips (maybe)
woodworker's glue
pliers

Directions:
1. Remove the legs from one colander.
2. Glue the porcelain seating into the bottom of the other (legs-on)

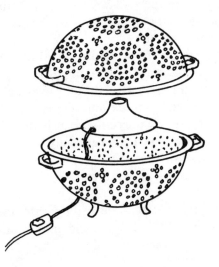

colander, bringing the cord from the socket out through one of the holes in the colander.

3. Screw a bulb into the socket and then put the legless colander, upside down, on top of the first one. If it happens to be a bit larger than the first one, no problem. It will just sit there.

4. If the colanders are exactly the same size, fashion some braces to hold them together by their rims. The legs you took off the top colander may do it. If you can't bend them, try bending some paper clips into the shape of staples and working with them.

The on-off button outside the globe will save you from taking it apart every time you want to turn on the lamp. Light shining through the punched-out holes in the colanders is a nice decorative effect, besides lighting up a dark corner of your living room.

In enhancing the atmosphere in your living room, you are missing a good bet if you don't arrange for light to do more than a little of your decorating for you. The pin points of light in the shape of stars (or whatever) in the colander-globe lamp just mentioned is a most attractive focal point at night; but so is the design that sunlight casts on a white wall or ceiling through the slats of a venetian blind. When placing that Egyptian rattan screen, that peacock chair, that asparagus fern around the room, keep in mind their relationship to lighting, whether natural or artificial. You can get wonderful effects with shadow play. By simply flipping a switch at night you can cast lovely designs on wall and/or ceiling if lamps are placed in the right relationship to some objects of decoration. Wall lamps shining through a room divider can texture the wall beyond. Ceiling fixtures or floor lamps can create the illusion of a gorgeous wall hanging if their light is directed through some foliage.

There is an apartment on the second floor of a high rise in Manhattan's Kips Bay area that must be inhabited by very kindly or very burglar-shy people. Walking by at night and looking up at the windows of this apartment, you can see only the ceiling. Because of the lighting inside, what you see on the ceiling is a shadow design of plants and grasses and who-knows-what that is really something to behold. I often wonder if it's being stared at by someone inside the apartment or if it's strictly a benefit performance for passersby. Either way, it's to be admired.

A globe, simply hanging from the ceiling through a hole on a cord, is one of the principal forms of incidental lighting now rigorously espoused by contemporary designers; three in a row, with the globes at different heights, is even more "in." With this sort of tier in your living room, you don't have to worry about much additional lighting. One of the dangers with these globes on cords is that people itch to gussy them up with fancy shades of one kind or another. Try to resist this urge. If you can't, plain paper lantern shades, please, only.

Built-in shelving is a blessing. If you move into a house or apartment with lots of shelf space already in place, count yourself lucky. If not, and your living room is of any size at all, you will want some system of cabinets and shelves, either against a wall or as a room divider. These systems can, of course, be custom-built to fit your home—at enormous cost. They can be bought brand new in totally finished condition—the next most expensive way to do it. Or, they can be—in descending order of cost—bought unfinished but put together, bought in pieces and put together by you, picked up second-hand, salvaged free from some throw-out spot. It used to be that the budget decorator could just go down to the corner store and get unlimited numbers of orange crates and then go on to the back door of the factory or department store for a couple of pallets (those little wooden platforms that hold machinery or furniture for storage or transportation) and there would be a whole wallful of "modular units." I don't know about your neck of the woods, but in mine the storekeepers now are too smart to throw the fruit crates away, and those pallets go for about 4 dollars from a local secondhand wood dealer. Moreover, I recently saw in a department store some wood and metal milk-bottle containers for about 35 dollars each. This is another modular unit that used to be free for the asking. Consequently, things go a bit harder for the pennypinching do-it-yourselfer. Furniture makers today advertise wooden cubes and rectangles that can be put together in all sorts of arrangements—at exorbitant prices.

There is one good way to beat the racket, though, if you are not averse to sneaking furtively around the streets after shop-closing hours. The contemporary manifestation of the old orange crate is an open-topped, rigid plastic crate with handholds on the sides that is used by dairy foods wholesalers in making deliveries to their retail customers. For some reason many wholesalers don't pick up the empties when they make the next delivery; hence, a number of

these handy, strong boxes in various colors are to be found abandoned on the sidewalks at night in any city or town. Occasionally,
the retail shop operator will be lurking behind the door of his establishment to shout obscenities at you if you dare pick one up out of
the gutter; but this unpleasantness is rare. These nifty cartons can be
carried home, one by one, night after night, until you have the mak-
ings of a total wall unit. Fancy department stores and mail-order
houses sell a version of them, called Stow 'n' Go Boxes, for about 7
dollars apiece. Here are some other uses for these durable good-
looking crates:

home-office file case;
coffee-table bottom;
bookcase;
vegetable bin;
magazine rack;
record holder;
toy box;
dollhouse;
infant holder (on a sled or cart);
sewing basket (with a fabric lining);
general storage.

Put roller skates or casters under them and they will slide easily
from place to place. Paint them all one color if you don't fancy a
varicolored wall unit. Glue them together, wire them together, tie
them with string, or just pile them up without any permanent joining. Nail them to wood surfaces through their filigree sides with
large U-shape brads. These rugged crates are altogether ideal home
decorator's building blocks; when you spy one, work fast—the person behind you will grab it if you don't!

Speaking of "useful boxes to put things in," where would any
household be without a number of them? In fact, a house itself can
be thought of as a useful box to put things in. And we oughtn't to
be too hidebound about what kinds of boxes can handle what sorts of
things. Consider those wooden-dowel crates in which live poultry
is placed when driven to market. Picture this: a living room wall
lined with a grouping of these wooden poultry crates, stereo components in some, books in others, plants in others, bar equipment
in still others. It would definitely "work," combining good decoration with functionality.

Another useful agricultural sort of box is what I call a peach basket, that item shaped like a round-end shoe box. Fasten a group of them to one wall in a tier arrangement. Near the front door, they could hold scarves, gloves, keys, and some light sports equipment. Or, employ square berry boxes in the same way. Or, ranged along the top shelf of your wall unit, use them to hold all sorts of things: playing cards, other game pieces, paper clips, and rubber bands. At the age of seventy-five my father became a nonsmoker and a useful box was rendered useless. My mother, thinning out possessions, presented me with his ancient wood humidor and a collection of clay and briar pipes. So handsome a box was the humidor that I tried to bribe my husband by promising the whole works to him if he'd limit his smoking to the pipe. This ruse didn't work; he kept hoarding newborn-baby cigars in the moisturized cask. It moved around with us for some fifteen years, collecting cigars and dust. The other day we found a perfect purpose for the box, utilizing its white, smoked glass lining and showing off its pleasing dark brown finish, its graceful lines and rounded corners. It sits on the fireplace hob, holding two small plants, a coleus and a Christmas cactus.

"Container" is synonymous with "useful box"; and contain is just what a fireplace does, if it's a good, functional one. The fireplace is such an obvious and easy element of design in the room where most of your playing and working is done that you may have overlooked its versatility as a container. To contain a fire is its raison d'etre, of course, but when a burning log is not indicated, have you thought of filling the fireplace with plants? Or how about sculpture, natural or man-made? Some things not to fill it with—please, for esthetic reasons—is fake birch logs. Yes, they are manufactured in our funny old country, as well as phoney ashes for the floor, too!

Mantelpieces, when they exist, are natural collectors of objets d'art, whether bought, inherited, made yourself, or just picked up from field, stream, and city streets. Make a surprising mixture of things, such as a congeries of natural and contrived articles, pay off (decoratively speaking) on the mantel, a natural-born focal point. Here are some of my favorite items of mantelpiece art:

stones;

bones;

shells;

bird nests;

glass animals;
shellacked gourds;
driftwood sculpture;
pewter candlesticks;
hurricane lamps;
ceramic vase full of dried grasses;
the jawbone of an ass.

Displayed on a high mantelpiece of an eighteenth-century fire-place I know is, actually, the jawbone of an ass. Found in the side meadow of the farmhouse that boasts this mantel, it is more likely the jawbone, with several molars still in place, of a domestic horse or cow long buried, some of its bones recently surfacing. It may sound ghoulish, but this relic, whitened with age and splintered into interesting form, is a very exciting piece of natural sculpture. If you have anything that dramatic on the mantelpiece, it's probably best to go easy on the copper and silver, leaving space around it.

Traditional fireplaces can be given a very contemporary look, if this is your desire, by *removal* of the mantel. If you take off the mantel, the wall above becomes the place to hang your most prized painting or bas-relief. Tile around the fireplace opening, or wood-panel around it, or do both, to cover the place from which you removed the mantelpiece.

There is a lot to be said, particularly in the contemporary-style house, for the freestanding fireplace made of metal. It radiates its heat in several directions at once and provides a focal point nearly anywhere you choose to position it. This kind of fireplace can be suspended by its own flue from the ceiling, thus providing an additional safety feature: in the event of earthquake, the whole assembly swings and sways, saving the house from burning down!

Yes, a fireplace is a very good focal point; but, if your living room lacks one and your rented oil painting has just gone back to the public library (mine, incidentally, has a peachy collection of poster art for borrowing), how about putting up a fake stained glass window? This collage-work is very easy to do. First work out a design on paper, pencilling in the colors you hope to buy. Then buy the colored glass from a glazier or pick up a stained glass kit from an arts and crafts store. With one color of adhesive-backed tape, tape the pieces together onto a piece of very light plywood the same color as your wall. A "window" of this kind could provide you with a color scheme to build the rest of the decoration around. A geometric design of vari-colored squares and rectangles will save you from having to buy a glass-cutter, since colored glass is most often sold in 8-inch squares.

Besides libraries, by the way, smaller museums and galleries are good sources of rentable art. You don't always have to take the final step and lay out hard cash for a Dufy watercolor, and such places are good sources of "prints suitable for framing," *for free*. A catalog is the name of the game. One of the ways a gallery has of luring pro-spective buyers is to issue a splendidly printed catalog. Even if you're not a prospective owner of what's being shown, if you walk in look-ing and talking like one, you can often walk out with a collection in miniature of the etchings, oils, or whatever on display. I recently fashioned a stairway hanging by taping to the back of a piece of scrap Plexiglass a dozen fine little full-color prints of Asger Jorn oils, which are a torn-up catalog issued to interested friends by his dealer. It's a very cheerful (and costless—the Plexiglass was found in the dump) enhancer of that particular dark spot.

The Metropolitan Museum of Art in New York City, and I'm sure many other population center museums, market creditable repro-ductions of classic statuary. Such museums usually issue an annual or semiannual catalog, free or for a nominal charge, showing what reproductions will be available that season. This practice is worth bearing in mind when you look around your most lived-in room and see that it cries out for a handsome piece of sculpture. If you've saved enough money by making or renovating the principal pieces of fur-niture, you deserve to blow it on a casting of that tall-sitting Egyp-tian cat you've admired for centuries in the original or in photo-graphs. Buy her in bronze—you'll never regret it.

This brings us to the question of fauna in the living room, a touchy question when the animals are live. There are all those people with animal allergies who won't be your guests until poor little Fido or Cat Vonnegut Junior has been gone for six months and the place fumigated several times. These unfortunates usually don't object to a parakeet or canary in the corner, and some actually enjoy an aquar-ium in the middle of your room divider. But kind hospitality often requires us to keep furry pets in some other part of the house. If you're an animal lover you can live with this since fauna, like flora, has always been so much a part of the arts and crafts, too. Stuffed heads of moose or antelope coming out of the wall over the fireplace are an abomination; a hovering falcon under a glass dome is, thank goodness, no longer the average American's idea of what should be on the library table. But it is very much okay today for a horse of wrought iron, a goat of porcelain, a terra-cotta pig, a marble frog, an aluminum armadillo, or a wood-sculptured rhinoceros to provide one of your room's focal points. So popular have those little end tables made of wicker elephants become that they are almost a decorating cliché. Despite my fondness for wickerware, I wouldn't have one in the house if it were given to me. But, if anyone wanted to present me with one of those wicker monkeys that approach the same state of banality, I'd immediately hang him by his long arm from the beam that crosses my living room.

Porcelain animals aren't as costly as you might imagine, depending, of course, on where you buy them. In Macy's recently I saw a lovely bear of porcelain about 12 inches high for 30 dollars. Alongside him was a 4-foot kangaroo in plastic chair-covering material, wearing a price tag something like 350 dollars. My immediate reaction was to ask why anyone, even given a certain kinkiness about kangaroos, would pay that price when he could so easily pay a dollar or so for a pattern of a toy kangaroo to stuff, enlarge it to the desired dimensions, and stuff it himself.

If you happen to have your own jigsaw in the basement, there's no limit to the number of plywood animals you can cut out. Stain or paint them, or cover them with fabric, and you can have a whole menagerie standing around your living room.

Since the living room is usually the sunniest room in the house, most of your houseplants will find themselves in this room. If possible, mass them all in one area of the room, or all but one. There's something sort of distracting and unrestful about a little fuchsia here, a tiny philodendron there, and potful of flowering begonia somewhere else, all equidistant from each other. They have an orphans-in-the-storm aspect. To get decorative mileage out of your plants, group them, whether in a window, on the floor, or on some sort of plant holder, or hanging. Suspending three or four plants, one above the other, from a skyhook makes a nice up-and-down effect. Study a macramé plant hanger in a shop window, then go home and tie some string together in the same way for your own homemade several-tier plant hanger. One of the advantages of this arrangement is that you need a moisture-catcher only on the bottom plant pot; and, since the sidewalks and dumps are full of discarded plastic plant holders that have lost their water-catcher bottoms, you can use these finds on the top levels.

Speaking of flora and fauna, I've always wanted to live in a house built around a great old tree, haven't you? Not a tree house (which is one built *in* a tree), but a house built with due respect to the ancient oak (or maple, redwood, sycamore, or whatever) that is the "previous tenant" of the piece of land on which the house-building is to take place. Far better than to raze an elm that has been leafing out for 150 springtimes would be to have the fun of decorating a living room with a sturdy tree trunk coming right up through its middle. I've seen one or two such rooms in my time, the bark-covered trunks providing both architectural elements and focal points. The owners of these homes have wisely refrained from gussying up their tree trunks with coats of paint or decorative hangings, preferring the stark beauty of the wood itself. (I think that I might not be able to restrain myself from building a round, or possible hexagonal, table of wood around the tree trunk.) And, of course, a tree in the parlor is a marvelous ice breaker and conversation piece.

As is the tombstone a magazine editor I know has in the living room of her New York City apartment. It isn't her gravestone, nor is it related to her in any way. She found it not among friends and relatives in a well-kept cemetery, but seemingly thrown away in a garbage dump in some upper New York State small town. Admiring its proportions and the crumbly look of the half-obliterated chiseling, she brought it home and gave it a place to rest in her parlor. Why not? It surely makes entering her room a unique experience.

You don't need to go that far in creating interest among the "things" in your main reception room. The 100 or more dollars that you would spend on a cigar store Indian or antique gum-ball machine would be better invested in basics. But I'm sure you've experienced, as I have, rooms that are so perfect, so unobjectionable, so fashionable that they are a bloody bore. They need some touch of irony, of incongruity, of novelty to pick them up. It can be a bowlful of Christmas tree ornaments left on a table year-round, or a weathervane used as a hat stand for guests (or just as a standing sculpture), or your collection of brass and ceramic doorknobs mounted on felt-covered plywood set on the piano . . . just something unexpected.

In my city apartment years ago the surprise was a little Victorian parlor organ. No, nobody in the family *played* it, but my husband and I hadn't been able to resist it at the first country auction we had ever attended. When we had not a stick of furniture to our names, what did we go out and buy? An organ, for heaven's sake, and three blue-and-white Meissen onion pattern plates. Well, you have to start somewhere! The melodian later became a desk.

Depending on your profession or life-style, a desk of some sort is essential in the living room, unless you have a study besides. A Chippendale secretary is dandy or a Queen Anne kneehole; so is an American nineteenth-century walnut rolltop. But these wonders are not for the likes of the low-budget decorator. A wooden flush door is, though; and it still makes one of the best working desk tops going around these days. Get a pair of two-drawer metal file cabinets from an office furniture sale, and you're all set. Or get one file case and support the other end of the door by two legs of the proper height. Sturdy cardboard mailing cylinders that you've strengthened with a coat of shellac, varnish, or polyurethane will do it. Or fasten one end of the flush door to a bookcase, room divider, or the wall itself. If your living room is also your study or office, you owe yourself this kind of a businesslike desk, especially if it will be typed on.

I make such a big point, so often, of wood furniture that you might think I feel it's the only material something like a desk can be made of. Not at all. I *do* love wood; there are good vibes in the look of a well-grained panel of golden oak, knotty pine, or teak. But, in some respects, wood is an unsatisfactory building material. It swells and shrinks with changes in the atmosphere, for example, as anyone knows who tries to close a cabinet door after thirty days of rain. Unless it's extremely hard wood, it bruises easily, and, of course, it burns with alacrity. In many ways the new plastics are far more satisfactory. In a house I was once "sitting" I worked for some months on a seamless, all-from-one-mold, white plastic desk with a trough-shaped groove in it for holding books, pencils, and other supplies. It couldn't have been a more comfortable, efficient, or attractive piece of furniture.

If your work (or avocation) does not require a desk top and the living room is the only room where you can do it, don't despair. Many kinds of arts, crafts, and occupations fit very well into the main room in your home, and the equipment essential to these pursuits is good decoration. Can you think of anything that has better lines than a harp or a pianoforte? If string quartet playing is your bag, don't, for goodness sake, "hide" your instrument. Fill the corner with it—even its case is good design. Some woodwinds are so beautiful in shape that, even though there's no musician in my home, I'd pick up a cornet or French horn if I found it cheap enough at an auction just to suspend from a beam or place on the mantelpiece. I have a friend whose living room is immeasurably improved by the presence of a xylophone behind the centrally placed divan. My niece's accordian contributes a conversation piece to my sister's otherwise rather forbiddingly formal parlor. A guitar and bongo drum over the fireplace are a sight prettier than two pistols and an air rifle.

A hooking frame is a good-looking piece of furniture; if there's a rug-in-progress on it, so much the better. A sculptor I know, who works small and boasts no separate studio, has his working materials set up right in his living room. A printer has a small, neat press in one corner of the dining room. Painters' easels in the company room don't seem to bother their "company." Many looms, for home weaving, are perfectly beautiful pieces of furniture. Should you find a big, old wooden loom at a country auction going for small dollars, buy it for that "unfurnished" corner of your L-shaped living room. Then teach yourself weaving, and soon you will be halfway through a runner for your center hall.

Like half the population, both male and female, of this country, are you into needlepoint or bargello? Then you don't need to be told how many different ways you can decorate with it. The chair seat or pillow cover is hardly the end of it. Have you considered that when you have finished your twelfth seat cover and twenty-fourth pillow sham, you could switch to something plain for the next batch of pillows and stitch the needlepoint units together into an area rug? I did that recently with hand-hooked chair-seat mats and it worked fine. They were round in the original, so I just sewed them to an old burlap curtain that had somehow survived several moves and deluges and filled in the background with plain black wool. That was a way of cheating on a hand-hooked rug (the chair seats had been done a million years ago by my mother), getting the feel of hooking, and gaining a new area rug all at the same time.

If Chinese checkers, parcheesi, or chess are very big at your house, why put away the board and pieces when the game is over? Backgammon boards are handsome and a chess set with well-made pieces is good decoration. Real buffs with more money than they know what to do with often commission sculptors to make them special sets. Whatever the form of relaxation and play, make it pay off for you in decorating.

Folding panel screens are very useful additions to most living rooms. They can hide ugly functional pieces, keep drafts from entering the room, hold photographs, prints, or other flat-art decoration, act as bulletin boards, cover a viewless window or a seldom-used doorway, or divide a large room into separate living-working-playing areas. Folding screens can be found thrown out in dumps or incinerator rooms. I still haven't forgiven an ex-landperson of mine for getting rid of a wood and monk's cloth one without first asking me if I wanted it. But they are also easy to make yourself. Here are a trio of simple-to-make panel screens.

How to Make a Folding Screen From Window Blinds

Materials and Tools Needed:
three window blinds (louvres) each about 70 × 18 inches
six metal hinges with accompanying screws
three pairs metal bookends
hammer
nails (some flat-headed)
screwdriver

Directions:
1. Pencil-mark the position of the metal hinges, three on each side edge of what will be the middle blind, equidistant from top and bottom of the blind and from one another.
2. Pencil-mark the position of the hinges on right-hand edge of the left-hand blind and left-hand edge of the right-hand blind to correspond with the marks you made on the middle blind.
3. Be sure you are applying hinges in the right directions, so that the panels will fold Z-fashion, rather than U-fashion.
4. Pencil-mark the positions of the three metal bookends on the bottoms of the three blinds, staggered a little so that when the screen is folded up they won't run into one another.
5. With hammer and nails, start the screw holes in middle blind.

6. Screw the hinges into place in the middle blind.
7. Repeat steps 5 and 6 with the two side blinds.
8. By hammering flat-headed nails around the edge of the metal bookend uprights into the wood at the bottom of the blinds, attach the "feet" to the three blinds, being sure the longer part of the bookend bottom is opposed on the two outside blinds: that is, that it extends outward in both directions when the screen is folded up.

How to Make a Folding Screen From Scrap Wood and Wallpaper

Materials and Tools Needed:
enough 2- × 2-foot wood to make three panels, each about 18 × 70 inches
enough wallpaper to wrap around and staple into the edges of these three panels
staple gun and staples
six metal hinges and accompanying hardware
hammer and nails
screwdriver
glue

Directions:
1. Cut the wood pieces into six lengths of 70 inches and six widths of 16 inches.
2. Nail the pieces together into three rectangular frames.
3. Wrap the wallpaper around each panel and press folds into it with your fingers.
4. Apply glue to the wood where the wallpaper will come into contact with it.
5. Wrap the wallpaper around the panels and allow the glue to harden.
6. Staple the wallpaper to the edges of the panels where it overlaps.
7. Now that you have made the three panels, proceed as in the project above, except substitute for the metal bookends feet made of three short pieces of wood scrap or furring nailed to the bottoms of the three panels.

How to Make a Folding Screen From Old Screen/Storm Doors

Materials and Tools Needed:
three wooden inserts of the same size from no-longer-used storm/
    screen doors
some fabric left over from your slipcovers
glue, needle and thread, or staple gun

Directions:
1. Where the screen is intact, simply cut the fabric to its size, hem
   the edges, and glue or sew the fabric into the panel. If you have
   enough fabric, back-to-back it.
2. Where the screen is no longer there, glue the fabric to the edge of
   the wooden panel. Or, better still, staple it in.
3. Now proceed as in the window-blind folding screen project on
   page 146 (again substituting wood-scrap feet for the metal
   bookends).

Using this general technique, you can think of dozens of raw materials to employ in this way. Three or four old wooden doors you
picked up in the dump could be put together into a dandy folding
screen. They don't have to be exactly the same width or length—
another case of not-quite-matching providing eye appeal above and
beyond what your standard mail-order catalog piece of furniture
can do. Three paneled wooden doors interspersed with two flush
lauan doors (a 16- by 80-inch brand-new set costs under 10 dollars

at a wood-supply store near me), for example, hinged in rickrack fashion, could divide a rather large room into study and "entertainment center."

I've saved until almost the end of the chapter the tricky question of how one fits the television into a decorating scheme. My answer is a complicated one. In the first place, the tube doesn't make a very good "focal point," at least not when it's turned off, so I happen to be of the opinion that the best thing to do with the TV-at-rest is hide it. I was recently in a most attractive late eighteenth-century house where this twentieth-century necessity was behind a panel in a handsome wormy-chestnut wall. One simply opens a "secret door" by a tiny knob when it's time to watch the evening news. In another such home the telly is fastened to a waist-high shelf on the inside of a deep coat closet door; open the door and the tube swings out into viewing position.

If you agree with my contention that your standard television set is one of the ugliest pieces of furniture we've yet come up with, perhaps you will find some merit in one of the following subterfuges:

have a cabinet with sliding panels constructed around it;

put it unobtrusively in a corner and place a three-panel folding screen around it;

suspend it from the ceiling on metal braces, and keep it decently draped when not in use, like a bird cage at night;

sink it into the place where the revolving works used to go in an upright player piano;

set it into the fireplace if a crackling fire on the grate is not your idea of home entertainment.

This last notion is a sensible one only if you have a raised fireplace. One really ought to look up a little at a television screen, or at least stare with the chin level, not buried in the chest (which is bad for the heart, lungs, and may lead to double chinnedness). Position the tube as high in the room as you can.

If you belong to the let-it-all-hang-out school, you probably have no vexation with TV placement. It simply goes on top of the only piece of furniture sturdy and deep enough to support it. A friend of mine living in a converted barn keeps his TV in the hayloft, from which it peers out, its rear end elevated a little to facilitate viewing it from a chair on the floor below. Another couple positions theirs on the tray of a Windsor (reproduction) high chair, a spiffy-looking piece of furniture given to their baby, who has far more efficient chairs to eat from. This is a nice example of decorating wittily with incongruity. Another might be to place the television set in a wood-burning stove, whether Franklin or one of those handsome new designs from Scandinavia. At this writing, a creditable American imitation of one of the Norwegian cast-iron boxwood heaters with excellent proportions is being advertised in the January sale of a Connecticut cut-rate chain. Regularly 89 dollars, this wood-burning stove is marked down to 66 dollars, a very good value. (The idea of switching to this kind of heating is clever in the present energy crisis. A book by Geri Harrington gives you the lowdown on all the various brands of wood burners available in this country.)

Happily, sound systems, even when stereo, are now built in such graceful and trim-size components that they don't present quite the same problem to the budget home-decorator as the TV set does. Installing components is definitely a do-it-yourself; don't be taken in by the proposition that only a sound expert can do the groundwork for filling your living room with canned music or getting the most out of your tapes.

If you *still* feel that there is one piece of furniture for your main room that you don't want to find, beg, borrow, steal, or make yourself, at least order one delivered to you in parts and put it together yourself. All sorts of furniture manufacturers and distributors now feature knockdown pieces, which cost far less than they would put together and delivered whole. Any period of style of furniture can now be ordered in this way—even Shaker reproductions. The saving is considerable, and the directions for assembling your table, desk, or chair are foolproof. If an early American hutch or dry sink is not what you are about to try building yourself, consider buying a knockdown one. Assembling it will ease you into home carpentry and will give you the same degree of satisfaction that making a cake from a mix does. *Then* you can think about what piece you will build yourself from the infallible directions in this book.

TIPS

- *If your baroque Madonna or Chagall print doesn't hang straight, and no amount of hand-straightening does it and if you don't want to disturb the permanent hanging job that's been done, tape a coin or metal washer to the back of the higher-hanging bottom corner.*

- *Antique shops or wrecking yards sometimes have miscellaneous-looking pieces of metal lying around collecting dust. If among these collections you can find an old fireback (the sheet or iron, usually, that used to be inserted into the back of the fireplace in earlier times), bring it home. It will improve the performance of your fireplace as a heating unit.*

- *Using a secondhand zipper that has slipped its mooring is a foolish economy. They never work right again once they've gone amok. Better invest in a new, working one.*

- *When measuring a piece of furniture for slipcovering material, measure only the parts that will show in the final construction. For undersides of cushions, backs that will be against the wall, etc., use old scraps from your rag bag.*

- *If you can't find ready-made welting in the color you want, you can easily make some yourself. Just cover some stout string or twine with the fabric of your choice, remembering to stitch the joined side with 1/4 inch or so extending beyond the stitching.*

- *Real leather is nifty: for chair seats, hassock covers, inlaid table and desk tops, among other uses. Man-made, leatherlike fabrics such as Naugahyde wear better, don't fade, mildew, or rot, and no animal had to die to provide them. Some of these miracle materials have been refined to such a degree that only a skin freak would really prefer "real" leather.*

- *Should you move into an apartment whose window problem is beat-up wood forming a valance or border around it, an elegant fabric glued to the wood may save the day.*

- *In repairing the underpinnings of a chair or couch, you'll find that an Afro comb makes a fair substitute for a webbing stretcher.*

- *Saving tacks removed from upholstery is a false economy. Any tack or nail that is bent is a sure candidate for the trash bin.*

- *Miniatures of larger objects make witty living-room decoration: a dollhouse-size trestle table on the trestle table, a tiny stoneware pitcher reflecting the big white one on the mantelpiece, etc. A scale model of the Old Colonial it inhabits makes a splendid conversation piece.*

7

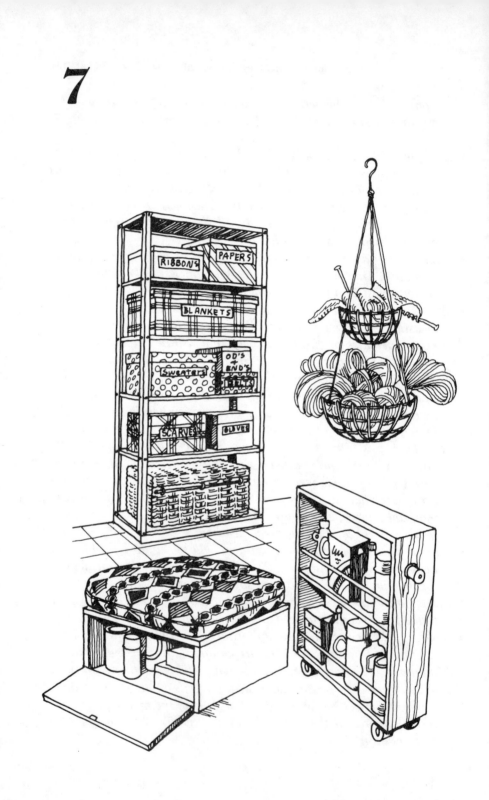

Room for Storage

If you're anything like me, moving—finally, after all those years of privation—into a *real house* with an *attic* can be dangerous. And acquiring a dwelling with both an attic and a cellar, fatal. There go all your good habits carefully developed over the decades of living with a minimum of *things*. Put an airtight waterproof attic in the hands of a natural-born scavenger and you know things are going to get collected in it. When I moved out of a house with a spacious attic, I had to hold a Tag Sale, after only six years of collecting. This institution, called in other parts of the country "Garage Sale," "Barn Sale," or "Yard Sale," is the favorite weekend diversion of numbers of people in my neck of the woods. The proceeds from my sale enabled me to move *and* pay the first six months' rent on my next abode; if I'd been equipped with a storage cellar, as well as an attic, perhaps my friends and neighbors (plus the weekending strangers who also turned up at my door on this historic occasion) would have taken care of my rent for the next *year* instead! With the exception of books, nearly all articles of home furnishing sold at my Tag Sale had been gifts from redecorating friends, pieces of junk picked up from sidewalks and incinerator rooms of large or small cities, items found in more than one town dump, or things bought years earlier (for pennies) at second-hand shops, wrecking yards, or other Tag Sales.

It was fun for a while not to have to figure out the clever use of very limited storage space; but it's just as exhilarating to discover ingenious means of utilizing the limited space one *does* have for putting things away. While the houses I've lived in for the last few years are atticless, one had a "box room," which is the charming term Europeans—and some Americans—employ for the catch-everything storage room, usually located on a high floor of the house. In my present home this catch-everything room is in the basement, which taxes my ingenuity, since items that might suffer from months of dampness can't be stored there. Metal would rust; wood warp; paper, cardboard, leather, fur, and fabric be subject to rot and mildew or acquire that cellar odor that is so hard to get rid of. Thus, following are some of the tricks I've learned through my vast experience of hating to part with things that "may come in handy some day." That day, by the way, is only too often just one removed from the Spring House-cleaning Day on which you threw them away.

"Fingers were made before forks," my brother used to say as he defied my parents, who were trying to instill some sort of a conception of table manners into the recalcitrant youth. And "Closets were made before neat, orderly, uncluttered rooms were considered a desideratum," I was about to aver. Then I remembered that the American Home in all periods before the Victorian never heard of a closet in every room. Classic Colonials seldom boast more than one closet per house, our forefathers presumably not believing in huge wardrobes. Or if they did, they had a piece of furniture (called an armoire or a wardrobe) built to hold their changes of costume.

We moderns, who usually enjoy a proliferation of closet space in our houses or apartments, sometimes fail to utilize to the utmost the space provided by this luxury. It offends my thrifty nature to see closet space wasted because it seems inaccessible to its owner: too high up, or too far back, or whatever. Behind the clothes-hanger pole in the front is where you put up a second pole (a discarded broomstick from a friendly garbage can will do it), and that's where you hang the off-season clothing that can't be packed away in boxes. On the top shelf, where you can't ordinarily reach just by stretching, is where those boxes go. There's usually a little waste space in a closet that is a foot or so wider than the width of the door or doors. The closet shelves usually traverse the length of the closet but fail to turn the corner and enable you to make use of this space to the right or left of the door opening. Without even going to the trouble of "building in" shelving, you can extend the ones that exist by placing pieces of scrap wood, plyboard, old bread boards, discarded grillwork, or some other kind of support in that space, anchoring it to the existing shelf by whatever you store in the corner.

Another way to extend closet storage space is the liberal use of cup-hooks on the backs of doors (or stick-on hooks on metal doors) or on beams and uprights in "unfinished" closets. Neckties (if you are, or live with, a man who still goes for them) make excellent closet "decoration" if hung on coat (or pants) hangers, which are then hung in tiers on closet doors or walls. Scarves or belts can decorate in this way, too, of course; or you can make an easy belt holder by screwing cup-hooks into the arms of a wooden coat hanger. If your closet is a deep one, don't neglect this bonus of space for storage on the back of the door.

If your master bedroom, as is so often the case in older houses, is a long narrow closetlike affair, why not create a clothes closet at one end of the room by stretching a pole, shower curtain rod, or broom-

stick clear across the end of the room. If you don't want to go to the expense of calling in a carpenter, but you don't consider the garments themselves sufficient decoration for that end of the room, affix a second rod in front of the one on which hangers will go, but up a bit higher, and hang on it curtains that will reach the floor. You could even attach a drapery track to the ceiling and use one of those gismoes by which you pull a string on the wall side of the drapes to open your "closet"; or you could open the closet by hanging the drapes on a pair of swing-away curtain rods. A missing walk-in closet with sliding wooden doors is not to be mourned when you can so easily make a capacious closet in this way.

If you have a space in one corner of the bedroom that is narrower than the width of the rest of the room and is not the desk or dressing-table nook, you can turn that into a clothes closet even more easily than the tricks outlined above. Sometimes the intrusion of a central chimney, an added bathroom, or other architectural feature creates a space at one end of a bedroom that can be turned into a clothes closet by the following method.

How to Turn a Nook Into a Closet with a Window Shade

Materials and Tools Needed:
two 3/4-inch boards, 4 inches wide and as long as the depth of your "nook"
woodworker's glue
pad saw
two lengths of shower-curtain rod, 1/2 inch shorter than the width of the nook
one window shade about 7 feet long and 1 inch shorter in width than the width of the nook
window shade-mounting hardware

Directions:
1. On the first piece of 3/4-inch board fasten one piece of window shade hardware—the little metal cup that holds one side of the shade rod—1 inch in both directions in from one corner of the board.
2. Measuring in 2 inches in both directions at the other corner on the same long side, mark a circle of a little longer diameter than the diameter of the shower curtain rod.

3. Now mark a similar circle in the very center of the board.
4. Saw out the two circles of wood.
5. Repeat steps 1 through 4 on the second 3/4-inch board.
6. Mark lines on both side walls of nook at the level where you want top of boards to come. (Measure the length of your longest garment and position hanger rod a few inches higher.)
7. Apply glue to the side of each board that will go on the wall.
8. Insert the two lengths of shower curtain rod through the holes made for them in the boards.
9. Press boards against walls and window shade mountings to the rear; hold them in place for a few minutes by hand.
10. Allow the glue to dry and harden for a few hours or overnight.
11. Install rolled-up window shade at back of boards.
12. Pull window shade across top of closet, over front rod, and down towards the floor, to close; to open your new closet, raise the window shade to an inch or so below front rod. The rod halfway back is, of course, to hang garments on.

These ways of creating storage space needn't, of course, be limited to the bedroom. They can work just as well in bathroom, kitchen, playroom, back or front hall, living room, or wherever there is a wall not holding up a major appliance or piece of furniture. What's behind curtains or shade, naturally, may differ from room to room: storage shelves, stacked boxes, or whatever. If the curtained closet is in a cellar or basement room—any space with at least one of its walls underground—be sure that what is stored there is done up in airtight packages, unless it's made of plastic, which is just about the only material that is mildew-proof.

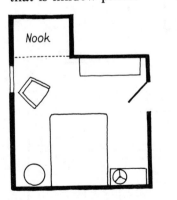

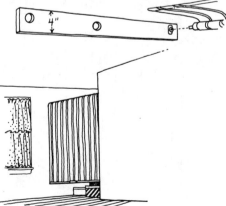

If you live in a house with more than one floor—or even a duplex apartment—there's one nifty storage space that I'll bet you're not putting to its optimum use. That place is under the staircase, frequently a neglected area. Sometimes smart budget decorators put washing machines there (louvered or venetian-blinded off), or sound systems, or even a lavatory. Occasionally, that triangular space is partitioned off, given a door, and made into a closet. But you don't have to go to those lengths to convert 'neath-the-stairs to excellent storage. Shelves can go in there, of course; one clever penny- and space-pinching notion is to stow all pots and pans and other cookware on open shelves underneath the back stairs out of the kitchen. Or how about building a little pyramid of cardboard cylinders (I don't know what comes in them, but you can often find such tubes around building sites or thrown away on city sidewalks)? Glue them together, or bolt them together; then give them extra durability by shellacking or varnishing inside and out. Such a storage unit could hold nearly anything you wanted it to. Here are a few possibilities:

pots and pans;
linens and towels;
toys and games;
shoes and boots;

hats and gloves;
other outerwear;
gardening tools;
pet foods;
bottles of wine;
or you name it.

The stairs themselves, which provide such interesting spaces to put things in, under or upon, are often overlooked as an item of decoration. You don't have to be the proud possessor of a long, gracefully curving stairway with a landing ample enough for two to duel on to see that your means of getting from one floor to another is handsome as well as utilitarian. One way to decorate, if the staircase is wide enough, is to put houseplants in pots along the first four or five risers, at one outer edge. Or cut flowers in matching vases; a set of glass beer steins, for example, could be very effective used in this way. If you work downstairs but file upstairs, you may find that between the balusters of the staircase is where file folders are often stuck for hours or days at a time. Why not cover some very stiff file folders with attractive fabric and let the edge of the stairway function permanently as a filing system? Or use it as a magazine rack, if you tend to collect periodicals to a large population before carting them off to the recycling center.

If additional floor and air space is what you're aiming for in remodeling, by the way, consider installing an iron spiral staircase. They are surprisingly modest in price, particularly at wrecking yards, but even bought new. The iron staircase provides decorative interest, as well as not chopping up your living space as much.

A man I know, with the object of creating more room on the upper level of his early-nineteenth-century house, relocated the stairway, equipping it with a both useful and good-looking rope banister. Then he had a tiny, narrow, steep, leftover wooden staircase going up to the ceiling and ending there on one side of his living room. Rather than rip out this "period" relic, he chose to leave it in place and use it for shelving. Books would have been my first thought; but he chose to display there his large collection of surrealist sculpture, mingling on each step with beautiful rocks and preColumbian figures. It's an imaginative way to "use" what would strike some people as a wholly superfluous vestigial remainder.

Storage places par excellence are made by picking up old school

lockers—those tall, skinny metal monstrosities—at junkyards or secondhand shops. It's a simple matter to put in shelves that fit what you want to store in them and paint them in enamel to fit into whatever room you need them in.

In your search for the perfect place for everything, have you ever considered roller skates? Or casters? Little wheels under things make it possible to utilize space for storage that you might never have thought of. When your file cabinets are filled to overflowing, spill the contents over into plastic milk cartons (like those mentioned on page 137) and stow them underneath your flush-door desk. The only trouble with this system is that to get anything into or out of the file you have to crawl under the desk with flashlight in hand—but for the roller skates you have under the cartons, which enable you to roll the files out into the open and the light.

The same principle can be applied to odd little spaces that are present in any room in the house. Take, for example, a narrow up-and-down space between a cabinet and refrigerator in the kitchen. Especially if your kitchen is a small one, that's space that need not be wasted. Why not make from scrapwood a narrow little herb-and-spice shelf that can roll in and out of that cubbyhole on wheels? Attach a wooden spoon or an empty thread spool for a knob onto the front and roll away—out of sight, out of mind, when you're not cooking with spices and herbs. The seasonings will retain their flavor and potency longer than if you "stored" them along the window sash. If there is a somewhat wider space on the other side of the refrigerator,

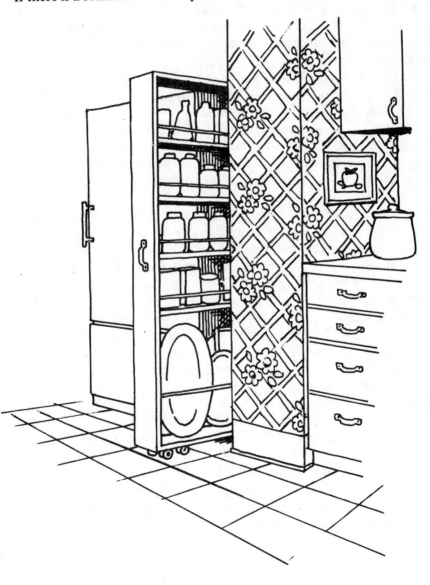

you can do the same thing there and use it for canned and bottled foodstuffs.

It seems to be a pet peeve of a good many interior designers that an inch or so of space is often wasted in the kitchen between the top of the refrigerator and the bottom of the cabinet over this piece of essential equipment. Look on top of your refrigerator; is there a 2- or 3-inch space that should have been added to the cabinet suspended above it? This is a good place to store trays or large flat dishes. If low heat rises from the back of the refrigerator, it may be a good place to dry freshly gathered herbs, between two paper towels and on a metal tray.

Those odd, hard-to-reach spaces in corner kitchen cabinets can be used for storage of foods and utensils by the installation of a sort of lazy Susan shelf that turns around. A company with the trade name of Rubbermaid, for one, makes this kind of space utilizer in plastic; they also manufacture a slide-out tray that can be installed in deep kitchen cabinets so that you can get to the baked beans stored in the back without removing all the tuna fish and sardines in the front.

Other places where storage space is often wasted, neglected, or just not noticed in the average-size home are:

underneath beds or couches (flat boxes slide in so handily and even off-season bedding can be simply wrapped in dustproof plastic or paper);

under the bathroom sink (a perfect spot for shelving made of small boxes on their sides, one on top of the other);

inside suitcases (unless you have a series of ever-diminishing suit-cases that fit one inside the other, when you're not traveling is when your valises ought to hold off-season clothes, pillows, bedding, or whatnot);

under eaves (storage containers don't have to be triangular, only small, and another clever storage bin for under stairs or eaves is made by cutting off the top of a packing box or carton at an angle.)

But the prize for "most overlooked" probably goes to the space up high in most houses or apartments—underneath the ceilings. In many kitchens there's a wasted storage space between the top of the refrigerator or cabinets and the ceiling; in the bathroom it's the space over the bathtub. In many other rooms it's easy to build a shelf over a door frame or a window. One dining room arrangement for not wasting storage space is an open shelf attached to the wall, one foot below the ceiling, clear around all four sides of the room—a good place to store once-in-a-while china or glassware.

If you have a particularly high-studded bedroom, consider hanging a cabinet just under the ceiling over the bed's head. You can display your collection of Victorian gee-gaws on the shelves (leaving the doors open of course); and to the bottom of the cabinet you can attach a rod with gathered fabric hanging down to the bed, providing a sort of headboard for a mattress-and-springs-type bed.

But there are easy and obvious uses for that space at the top of the room. Even more imaginative storage-cum-decoration devices use ropes and pulleys to "store" musical instruments or sports equipment on the ceiling. I have seen a pair of bicycles so deployed. Since the owners have wisely refrained from tricking out the wheels with colored lights (transforming bicycles into chandeliers), they are easily lowered to the floor and trundled out to the corridor and the elevator of a city apartment building for the weekend's cycling; the rest of the week they stay aloft.

If you're a nut for Ping-Pong and your boss has just switched to billiards and offered you the Ping-Pong table in his country garage, don't turn it down because of your crowded two-room flat. Hoist it to the ceiling with ropes, hooks, and pulleys for letting down right over the bed when you're due for a game of table tennis. For a place to store a toboggan, see page 129.

Storage space, like so many aspects of clever budget decorating, must be thought of in a flexible, adventuresome way. In a twelve-room Colonial with full attic and cellar and five walk-in closets, putting things away is no problem; but in the compact three-and-a-half room flat, storing can be a terrible problem, unless you exercise some ingenuity and creativity. Since having dinner party stem goblets has been a bugaboo for a number of apartment dwellers I've tried to help in the past, I'm going to provide two nifty little devices for storing stemware without taking the chance of shattering a half dozen goblets while rooting around in the back of the glass cabinet for them. Both objects are great space utilizers and either will preserve your crystal for longer than its natural life.

How to Transform a Bureau or Buffet Drawer Into a Stemware Rack

Materials and Tools Needed:
1/2-inch plywood plank of the same dimensions as the inside of the
  drawer (Naturally the drawer must be one deep enough to accommodate your stemware, so use your tallest goblet as a guide:
  the drawer should be at least 3/4 inch deeper than the height of the
  glass.)
pad saw
two small strips of wood, a little shorter than the measurement from
  front to back of inside of drawer
nails
felt fabric (enough to cover plywood)
woodworker's glue

Directions:
1. Mark circles on the plywood in various sizes to fit your goblets;
   holes should allow the bases to go through, but be smaller than
   the "bowls" of your stemware.
2. Cut out the holes with a saw.
3. Lay felt on the plywood and mark the fabric for cutting the edges
   and the circles.
4. Cut the felt to size and shape.
5. Glue felt to plywood on the side you will have facing up.
6. Nail the two small strips of wood to the inside of drawer, one at
   each end, halfway up, and parallel to drawer bottom.
7. Apply glue to the top edges of these little support boards.
8. Insert felt-topped rack into drawer so it rests on support boards.
9. Allow glue to harden for a few hours or overnight.
10. Put stemware into drawer, one goblet into each hole. Your crystal
    will be safe from shattering, as you can always reach any piece
    without disturbing or crunching it against any other.

How to Build a Ceiling Stemware Rack

Materials and Tools Needed:
3/8-inch plywood board, 21 × 25 inches
two metal brackets, about 26 inches long, with right-angle ends

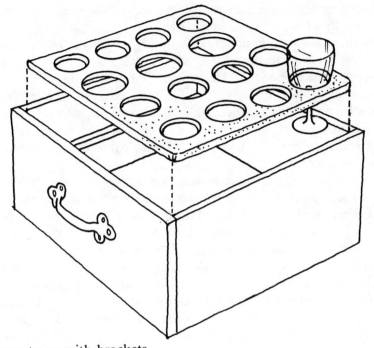

screws to go with brackets
screwdriver
saw
sandpaper
paint or enamel

Directions:
1. Starting from one corner of plywood board, measure along the longer side 3 1/2 inches and mark a short line at right angles to the edge.
2. Make a line parallel to the first one, 3/4 inch farther down the side.
3. Follow these first two marks with three similar pairs of lines, 3/4 inch apart, at 3 1/2-inch intervals.
4. Extend these lines to a length of 10 inches.
5. Starting from the corner diametrically opposite the one in step 1, repeat steps 1 through 4 on other side of board.
6. With a saw, cut out the eight grooves described by these lines.
7. Round off the corners of the groove "entrances" by sandpapering.

8. Measure halfway across the short sides of the board and mark screw holes for one end of each bracket.
9. Paint or enamel the nonbracket side of the board and the edges.
10. Screw brackets to the board.
11. Screw the other ends of the brackets into the ceiling.
12. Now slide your stemware, upside down, into the grooves, being careful not to overlap their bottoms. Your wine and water goblets will thus be safe from shattering and will always be available singly or in groups. And you will have composed an attractive ceiling decoration besides.

One of the things that the budget home decorator with plenty of storage space wants to do is never let a chance go by to visit the local dump, wherever he or she may be. Entire summer cottages have been furnished out of the town dump at Tisbury, Martha's Vineyard, an island off the Massachusetts Coast. "Summer people" at season's end make the most incredible discards, especially people who can afford to go to a summer resort, or a winter one, for that matter. I've also done very well in the landfill areas in places like Stowe, Vermont, or Franconia, New Hampshire. At the very least, you'll be able to keep yourself in firewood year-round. At the most, you'll also be able to cover your living room floor with a genuine Karastan rug (as a woman I know did after her weekly trip to a Rhode Island dump).

But you must develop your scavenger's eye: that odd-looking little metal doohickey may become part of a pin-up lamp you'll build next week; those curlicues of wood may serve as eye-catching brackets for the shelf-buffet you're putting up in the dining room. The junked blue jeans have enough intact fabric left in them to make a patchwork skirt for your double bed or a pillow sham. This particular penny-pincher keeps in the cellar storeroom not only baskets of wood "findings," and laundry bags full of miscellaneous bits of dress material, but ex-coffee cans and peanut butter jars labeled "Assorted Metal

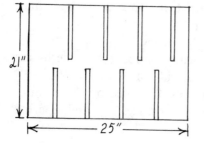

Parts," "Bits of Hard Rubber," or "Plastic Miscellany." I have no idea what some of these objects are, but you'd be amazed how often they have come in handy in creating some accessory or strange piece of furniture. You just can't tell when you'll want to dig into your mysterious collections to make that collage of found objects you've been thinking about. Mounted on a stiff cardboard (or thin plywood) it will be jim-dandy for hiding that cracked plaster spot on the living room wall. There are worse ways to spend a rainy afternoon.

TIPS

- *Ancient window shades tend to be worn out only on the bottom quarter or third, which is about how far most people have pulled them down over their windows. Trimming them of the faded, torn, or otherwise damaged portion and then moving the rein-forcement (sometimes wooden) up to a new "hem" can give you a perfect recycled window shade.*
- *Never pass by a lone glove you see lying on the street or sidewalk. The possessor of its mate will never return to the scene for it, and you can wear unmatched old gloves when you tackle your next staining or painting chore.*
- *Painting a staircase that is traveled several times a day is a problem. Solution: paint alternate treads on one day and the remaining treads the next day, or paint half of each stair tread the first day and the other half the second day.*
- *If there is a crack in a single pane of window glass, let its course determine the beginning of a leaded-glass-like design that you make across the pane with adhesive-backed tape. Or, press a group of butterflies you've caught, wing-tip-to-wing-tip, over the crack.*

8

Room for
Improvement

It is not necessarily, in the eyes of the world, an improvement to cover fumed-oak paneling with several coats of white paint. But the world's eyes aren't going to feast on those walls—*yours* are; and if glistening white (or ecru, lilac, or pistachio) paneling in the dining room is one of your longest cherished dreams, who's to say nay? If the paneling is not fumed oak, but that rather unpleasant tin stuff that looks a little like cookie cutters (which the Victorians seemed devoted to), the surface *would be* vastly improved by a coat of satin-finish paint. This gives the look of wood at about one-tenth the cost of ripping it out and installing wood paneling.

Camouflage and illusion play a major part in interior decoration; and the professional designer isn't the only one who can deal in these commodities. Study the walls of any room you are making your own to see what they need for eye appeal. If it is paneling and you lack the wherewithal to get a cabinetmaker in, you can simulate the effect of paneling in any number of low-cost ways. One is to get thin strips of half-round or other kinds of molding and make squares or oblongs of it on your walls. Glue the molding to the wall, using a woodworker's glue like epoxy or Elmer's, making sure that your corners are mitered. Then paint the wood trim either the same color as the wall or a contrasting color or glue fabric or wallpaper inside the panels. Or, here's a switch: with a limited amount of leftover wallpaper, use it on the parts of the wall that aren't panel and paint the panels and molding a color suggested by the wallpaper.

Beams can be "simulated" too. Fake uprights and cross beams, made of Styrofoam or some such plastic, are sold by the yard. Try to avoid these monstrosities. If "exposed beams" in a modern, dry-wall construction house are your heart's desire, please create the effect with some real wooden two-by-fours. Although plastic construction materials are far superior to their predecessors in a thousand instances, this simulated wood is not a shining example. I lived with it for a couple of years (in a rented house, naturally). Take my word for it: phoney beams are very depressing, besides the fact that they come unglued and fall away from walls and ceiling in a most unattractive manner.

Dry-wall construction simply means that the interior walls of your house are not brick, wood, or plaster. A dry wall is made of wallboard (gypsum board, plasterboard, Sheetrock, or fiberboard). This material takes very well to painting, papering, or covering with fabric. It's somewhat more difficult to remove old wall coverings from wallboard than from other kinds of walls. My advice is to wallpaper over existing paper, although some home craftsmen frown on this. If the paper seems ready to come off with ease, you're home free. Then a coat of sizing is desirable before applying your own new paper or fabric. Painting over old wallpaper you don't like produces a nice, soft finish; be sure in this case that you're putting a darker color over the colors in the wallpaper.

To help solve your paper-removing problems, there is a device called a wallpaper steaming machine. You can probably rent one from a paint and wallpaper establishment near you. I remember helping friends some years ago remove wallpaper in an old colonial house they had bought. We were using the soak-with-hot-water-then-scrape-scrape-scrape method. When we got down to the eleventh layer of wallpaper in one of the bedrooms, I wished for some such labor-saving device as a wallpaper steamer. The fun we had imagining the sorts of people through the generations who had used the various papers didn't really justify the tired arms and aching backs. Arriving at the eleventh—and last—layer, we left it on; it was probably the only thing that held the ancient plaster together!

The best thing to do with a tilting wall—next to ignoring it, that is—is to drape it. Draping an entire wall may also be a means of camouflaging oddly placed windows. If there's molding at the top of the wall, you can attach fabric to that; if not, stretch a curtain rod clear across the wall where it meets the ceiling. This operation also provides a good baffle for your sound system.

Sometimes plaster walls develop cracks that keep recurring no matter how many times you spackle and paint them over. There was one such crack in the ground-floor hall of a house I once rented.

That Rio Grande kept coming back to the wall, tracing an identical course in each layer of remedial plaster I applied—something to do with the fireplace upstairs and stresses and strains that would not be denied. I finally gave up and covered the crack with an obi (Japanese sash) I'd been hoarding for years, not knowing what to use it for but loath to discard such a good-looking piece of closely woven silk. It worked fine; and at last I knew why I'd been saving that sash so long.

Ever since as a weekend guest I shingled an exterior wall of a friend's house in the hills of Hurley, New York, I've been wanting to do some more shingling. It's great fun, it goes very fast, and, after an hour or so, you have a tremendous sense of accomplishment. On my last trip to my village dump, I found a whole flock of cedar shakes (shingles) thrown away. I can't understand this profligracy, since, if nothing more, shakes are great kindling. (Perhaps the caster-away lives in a fireplace- or wood-stove-less house.) Now I am going to get my chance to do some more shingling, but *inside* the house. These shingles will form one wall of the lavatory I'm building in the basement. I shall nail them right to the wallboard (also found in the dump) on that side of the small room. Why don't you see if there's a likely wall in some room of your house that would be improved by the application of shingles? Remember that they are not for exteriors only.

Likewise for clapboards. A crumbling wall in bedroom, living room, dining room, or kitchen could be nicely covered with clapboards, whether old-fashioned wood or newfangled aluminum siding. One often sees rooms that have been added onto existing houses with one wall of the singles or clapboards that were the original exterior. Why not treat a wall this way in the first place?

Or, you might want to fence a wall that has seen better days. A stockade fence along a wall in a not very formal room (perhaps a boy's bedroom) would be clever and attractive. A girl's room might benefit from a bit of picket fence; if you have some left over after treating one wall with the fencing, make a headboard for her bed. Besides covering the lower half of an imperfect wall, a picket fence can be used by Little Sister to perch stuffed animals, dolls, hats and scarves, and mittens upon. Even plain yeomanly snow fencing can be used effectively inside, simultaneously disguising beat-up walls and providing eye appeal.

Carpeting a wall may sound like a contradiction in terms to you,

but it might be exactly the thing to do. If, for example, you are faced with a cement wall, as in a basement room, where you desire warmth, texture, and insulation, try covering the wall with carpeting. The kind that can be bought (or found) in segments is easy to install. It needn't be all of the same color or pattern; try making a random pattern of two different solid colors. Fasten it to the wall with glue or with double-faced pressure-sensitive tape; and see how much better your chamber music records sound in this room now.

Have you thought of decorating a wall (and, incidentally, obscuring some of its imperfections) with a striking scarf? Some scarves are so utterly beautiful when spread out that it seems a shame to hide their virtues by scrunching them up around your neck. You can tack or staple a scarf to the back of a picture frame; you can glue or push-pin it directly to the wall. India print bedspreads used as wall coverings are, of course, an old trick, but why limit it to India print? Perhaps that patchwork quilt would look better on the wall than on the bed — or that colorful Mexican serape you've been using these several years as a couch cover. Sew the top of it to a metal or wooden rod that can be held by two or three hooks high up on the wall or suspend it by clip-on curtain rings to a cross-the-wall curtain rod.

Put latticework over a wall that is not all it should be. Besides an interesting textural effect, it has the added advantage of allowing you to hang things from it: plants in hanging pots, cooking utensils, clothing accessories, or whatever. Or, if not latticework, try a few slender laths, evenly spaced as uprights across the wall and fastened in place with woodworker's glue for a board-and-batten effect. The offensive proportions of a small, narrow, high-ceilinged room can be ameliorated (or seem to be—illusion again) by gluing a series of laths to one wall horizontally. Any one of the treatments in this paragraph applied to a wallboard partition will facilitate the hanging of mirrors, metal sculptures, or other decorative accessories too heavy for simple wallboard to support.

If the floor in one room of your house tilts or slants slightly, count yourself lucky. Do you know that in striving for authenticity in good

reproductions, some house builders actually *build in* slanting floors? I can accept this oddity, as I'm rather fond of a certain amount of incline in some floors (something to do with a sentimental attachment to a favorite aunt and uncle, whose dining room floor was 1 foot higher on one side of the room than on its opposite). But, if none of this cuts any ice with you, why not "correct" the situation by laying new floorboards, buttressed on the lower side by a lift of supporting boards? If you can pick up some flooring cheap because it's not all the same length of board, consider laying the floor diagonally instead of four-square. This makes a most interesting floor, as it does wall paneling.

Another possibility is to create interest underfoot by laying the new floor on only part of the room, making a platform across one end of the room. A writer I know did this (*did it himself*, though before this venture into home improvement he considered himself all thumbs). The result was that he could then see out of a too-high-up window as he sat on his platform at his typewriter.

There's nothing more beautiful than a floor of hardwood boards scraped down to a satin smoothness and then rubbed with a little oil now and again. But an undistinguished wooden floor can be a decorative asset, too. Seal it with a wood sealer and then paint it over a good, rich dark color. You might consider sponge-stippling it with a contrasting lighter color. This is very good for hiding blemishes and lends eye appeal to some wood floors. It's best to keep walls and ceilings plain in a room so floored or else the total effect may be too "busy."

Should you move in upon floors covered with terrible old moth-eaten linoleum or some other type of surface that you can't stand, your problem is less serious than with, say, a sagging ceiling. In the first place, the law of gravity is on your side; in the second, the floor covering of your choice, whether wood, tile, stone, or fabric, can be laid right over whatever is there now. Leave the moldy old linoleum there for extra insulation (and squeak-proofing). It's sometimes more trouble to get up and more damaging to the supporting timbers than it is to leave it on. If the basic flooring is cement, brick, or stone, you will want as many layers as is feasible before the one you'll actually walk on.

If you've moved into a house or apartment with wall-to-wall carpeting already down and wall-to-wall is an anathema to you, don't rip it up. There's probably a good reason it is there, such as an unfinished flooring underneath. The carpeting may be faded and/or spotted or it may not be to your taste, but there's no prohibition to laying your own large Oriental or scatter rugs on top of the carpeting. This will make an even more comfortable walking surface and will cover the imperfections at the same time.

Large department stores and floor-covering emporia often have sales of carpeting samples—little rectangles of carpet materials for 25 or 50 cents apiece. You can't make up a wall-to-wall carpet all in a nice dark turkey red for the library floor from these squares or rectangles, as they are in a variety of colors, textures, and patterns. But wouldn't it be a good, inexpensive way to carpet a small room floor, for instance a bath, entry hall, or small bedroom? A rug made up of twenty-four samples, 14 by 24 inches, would be very appropriate for a casual room. And it would have cost you under 7 dollars. Samples in different sizes can be put together for an interesting patchwork effect. You don't even have to sew them together: work out your design on the floor and then glue the separate segments onto a piece of felt or latex. A 10-foot round rug, made up of a patchwork mosaic of varicolored carpeting samples in rainbow hues, provides the floor covering in the main room of a very posh converted barn I know of.

What you find underneath a decaying wooden or linoleum floor, sometimes, is cement, as I discovered recently in a ground-floor "family room" of a converted barn. This portion of flooring was adjacent to a large corner fieldstone fireplace. My client and I decided that eventually we would lay building bricks on the area, but we wanted the time to locate the chimney remnant of a burned-down 19th-century house—or other cache of nicely weathered old bricks— which we would lay in a fan-shaped pattern at fireside. Thus, in the meantime, we *painted* right on the discolored old cement a design of brickwork and mortar. This accomplished two ends: first a decorative trompe l'oeil effect covering an unsightly floor; second the pattern all ready for laying the chimney bricks as soon as we found them.

Acquiring enough rugs for a large house is no problem even to a low budget, if you are a braider or a hooker. But you may not realize that dandy rugs (especially for summer seasons or warm climates) can be made from discarded nylon stockings and panty hose. Cut the elastic waistband off the panty hose and split each pair into two long "stockings." Then stitch your collection together into three very long strands and braid them. This is quicker by far, not to mention easier and cheaper, than making tubes of wool or cotton, stuffing them with cotton or kapok, and then braiding. Ask all your friends and relatives to save you their no-longer-wearable nylons and you'll soon have a bagful. An average-size laundry bagful will make a round rug 3 to 4 feet in diameter.

If your wealthy cousin has given you a slightly worn, long hall runner and your house lacks a long, narrow corridor, look around for a part of a room it could improve, either as it is, or cut into shorter lengths. It may be that you can improve the stairway with the runner. Just stretch it over the whole staircase, fitting it snugly into the angles, and nail, tack, or staple it at top and bottom of the risers. Quarter rounds of wood nailed through the carpet, just under the edge of each overhanging tread, are another way to do it.

If you *have* a long, narrow corridor (and no wealthy, redecorating cousin) that you are required by lease to keep covered, I have a suggestion. A floor covering that will wear like iron and that will save you from complaints from the downstairs neighbors if boisterous play takes place in the hall is cocoa matting or springboard covering. See the *Yellow Pages* of your telephone directory; the supplier may even deliver. The springboard covering with which I had a corridor covered for twenty years was so hard and durable that the cats walked carefully on the inch-and-a-half of floor space between the rug and the wall; people in bare feet would have, too, if they could have managed.

If you like the grain of your wood floor, but not its color, have you considered dyeing it? Wood surfaces can be dyed with ordinary fabric dyes. Prepare the dye bath in much the same way as you would for tinting fabric; make the solution somewhat stronger than for a garment. Bring the solution to a boil and slather it on floorboards with an ordinary paintbrush. Don't seal the wood first—it should be somewhat porous, rather than presenting a slick surface—as you want the dye to sink into the wood a little. As in coloring your curtains, bear in mind that the floor will dry a bit lighter than the shade it turns as you apply the dye. This method of coloring a floor will cost a lot less than urethane stain, latex, or oil paint. Wicker and basketry can also be dyed this way. So can rush chair seats: scratch up the surface if it's ever had any shellac or varnish on it. Don't try this with cane seating, which is too slippery a surface and too much trouble to steel-wool or sand down.

Dramatic effects with floors can be achieved by replacing worn-out or imperfect sections with contrasting materials. Brick in a corner where constant walking is not done; lay ceramic tile in a section under a window where you may want to place plants; alternate boards of contrasting colors; replace squares of worn-down vinyl with squares of high-nap broadloom. These are all possibilities.

Defects in ceilings should be corrected early, or else you may have a lawsuit on your hands. Plaster actually does fall on people's heads sometimes. Don't ever move into a house or apartment with dubious ceilings; have a builder check it out and determine whether it's a serious threat or just some simple flaking on an otherwise sound topside. If the latter is true, you can do it over yourself by scraping and then painting or even papering or gluing up fabric. In the illusion department, bear in mind that low ceilings can be lifted with light colors, while darker shades tend to lower a very high ceiling.

False ceilings are easily put up by amateurs; they can muffle light fixtures, softening the illumination and creating interesting patterns of light and shadow. Here are some suggestions for false ceilings that can improve the look of the top of your room:

plastic grillwork;

wooden latticework;

acoustical tiles;

parallel dowels;

a mosaic of ceiling board;

a collection of cardboard egg cartons glued together, cup side down;

a group of tin cans, ends removed, sides of cylinders glued or bolted to one another.

This last suggestion may sound unlikely; it's not. I've seen it done in a modern-decor apartment, and the streamlined effect is stunningly handsome, as is an attic playroom whose ceiling I was asked to "improve." In a big square house with a big square attic under a hip roof the ceiling was covered with yards of bright yellow-and-white striped canvas. It was fastened to the pinnacle with a light fixture, coming down on all four sides like a circus tent top. This treatment makes surprisingly good insulation and very handsome decoration.

If your ceiling is in pretty good shape—either plaster or ceiling board—but displays several spots that resist scrubbing, consider simply covering the spots with a painted-on geometric shape, with fabric, or with wallpaper. Case the leftover quarter-rolls of wallpaper left on the closet shelf by the previous tenant. If there is some that matches the paper on the room's walls, you can cut sections out—perhaps a flower formation or other figure—and simply paste them over the offending spots on the ceiling. If the wallpaper is striped, you may need only to cut out one or two stripes, which are far easier to fasten to the ceiling than is a whole width. With this method you will have "coordinated" the room's decor while disguising its imperfections.

For unaccountable reasons probably somehow related to the previous small, furry residents of my new house, large irregular holes were gouged in the fiberboard ceiling of the ground-floor study. Just now, while sauntering back from feeding the hens, I figured out how

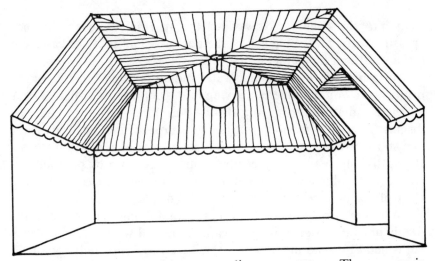

to repair this damage without spending any money. The answer is don't repair it. Just cover up the holes with a Mondrianlike pattern of strips of leftover wallpaper matching the walls in the next room. Where do the hens come in? Over the wallpaper strips, for textural interest and to keep the wallpaper in that somewhat damp atmosphere from coming unglued and falling down, will be panels of small-holed chicken wire. If you are not blessed with rolls of extra chicken wire in your backyard, check out your local hardware store (cut-rate, naturally); you'd be surprised how inexpensive this excellent decorating material is.

An inconvenient wall between kitchen and dining room can create extra steps when you're trying to get the meal on the table. Why not cut out a pass-through, a hole in the wall with its bottom edge at waist level, making sort of an interior window? It's easily done, especially with older walls. Just be sure you establish the hole *between* the wall's uprights, whether they be wood, steel, or concrete. Once you've got the opening cut through, you may find you can insert small boards in the side spaces between the walls to the two rooms. The boards can be used as shelves for salt and pepper, sugar bowls, and that sort of thing. Use an old breadboard for the waist-high surface, supporting it on either side of the wall with metal brackets, and there you go. Interior decorators have been known to do this sort of improvement for clients. One such operation on a very thick Park-Avenue-apartment wall provided a perfect serving surface. Rather than a breadboard, the decorator sank a pair of hot-trays right into the opening. Now when the apartment's tenant finishes "passing through," she plugs in the hot-trays and puts the casserole dishes on them for guests to help themselves.

Old-fashioned steam or hot-water radiators often present vexing problems to young moderns moving into older houses or flats. Don't let these radiators throw you; there are all kinds of ways to hide or disguise a radiator without sacrificing its proper function. The easiest and most obvious is to paint it the same color as the wall it's near. If you like its shape, on the other hand, play it up by painting it a contrasting color and then adding a shelf in the same color. On the shelf place some heatproof "focal point" display object.

Radiators are hidden sometimes with folding screens of some diaphanous material. Low ones can be masked with seating benches with metal or cane mesh sides. And here is an easy radiator shield you can make yourself; to conceal without obliterating its function, a radiator that stands against the wall to a height of three feet.

How to Build a Radiator Shield of Wood and Twine

Material and Tools Needed:
one 3/4-inch wood plank 10 × 20 inches
four 2 × 2s, 37 inches long
one 2 × 2, 16 inches long
two 2 × 2s, 6 inches long
a ball of twine
drill and drill bit
woodworker's glue

Directions:
1. Select a drill bit that will make a hole large enough to accommodate the twine without too much squeezing.
2. Around three sides (two short and one long) of the 3/4-inch board and 3/4 inch in from the edge, mark drill holes 1/2 inch apart, skipping 2 inches at each side of the corners.
3. Drill holes clear through the board at right angles.
4. Hold the 16-inch 2 by 2 against the long side of the shelf board you just drilled, their sides flush, and mark drill locations with a slender marker through the drilled holes on the 16-inch board.
5. Repeat step 4 using the ends of the shelf board and the two 6-inch 2 by 2s.

6. Drill holes through these three 2 by 2s *diagonally*, so the hole goes through the inside top corner edge of the boards.
7. Construct the frame by gluing the 2 by 2s together in the manner shown in the illustration. Make sure the diagonally drilled holes are on the inside top edges of the horizontal 2 by 2s.
8. Apply glue to the top exposed edges of the upright 2 by 2s and fix the shelf board to these four locations.
9. Allow to dry and harden overnight.
10. Starting at one bottom back corner of the construction, thread the string through the first diagonal hole and then up to the corresponding hole in the shelf board, down through the next hole in the shelf to the next diagonal hole in the 2 by 2.
11. Continue until you have the whole side finished; then start on the other side at the back bottom corner.
12. Using this same technique, fill in the front of the radiator shield with string.

You have now put together with a bit of string and some scraps of wood a handsome radiator camouflage that will blend in with any kind of decor.

If you move your office into your home and feel that the furnishings are too "officey," there are a number of things you can do to improve the situation. A good utilitarian desk is a good utilitarian desk anywhere it finds itself; but the metal file case moves into a parlor better if you paint it some blending-in color, wallpaper it in part or in whole, or even cover it with fabric to match some slipcover or other. Same goes for those horrid black or gray metal bookends and in-and-out boxes that are so useful; they're nonetheless

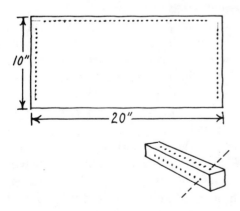
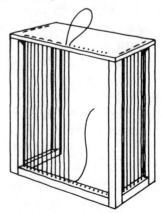

functional if the gun-metal curse is taken off them by some cheerful coloring. Putting your most active file folders on the desk top in an extra dish drainer works wonders, as does a little contact paper on an index-card-size file box.

Wallpapering a bulletin board to match the wall it's on improves things, too. Or, use the bulletin board to frame your favorite print and make a new bulletin board out of an old picture frame or removable part from a storm-screen door and an inset of felt-covered cardboard. Such a bulletin board, with fabric of a bright lime green, lights up the darkest corner of my living room, just to the hinge side of the entrance door. It's where I put up greeting cards from friends, reminders of what the oil company salesman looks like, and essentials of that kind.

The alteration of furniture other than office stuff is just as often accomplished by subtracting, rather than adding things to it to improve its appearance. A coat of paint or a covering of fabric is an easy quick trick, but remember the difference it made when you simply sawed the curlicue top off that Victorian bookcase and let the spines of the books themselves provide the "decoration"? Or, remember when you removed the canopy from grandmother's four-poster bed and gained all the lovely space at the top of the room? Study carefully those ungainly old armchairs to see which one could profitably lose its arms and become a side chair, slipper chair, or straight chair. You must ascertain that taking off the arms won't interfere with the chair's basic construction and stability. Tabletops that lose their awkwardly placed legs can still function nicely as tables with the addition of a central pedestal. (Wooden or metal pedestals are usually easy to find in wrecking yards.) A table of ungainly height can be converted to a coffee table by shortening its legs or its pedestal. A normal chair can, by the same method, be made into an accompaniment for a child's desk. Deleting fringe from the bottoms of chairs, couches, lampshades, or whatever is almost always a step in the right direction.

Should you move into a vintage building where the principal room has a Casablanca fan suspended from the ceiling, you may be tempted to tear out this fixture and replace it with something more contemporary looking. Think twice. These fans, some with lighting attached, are considered very "now," and sell for well over 100 dollars each. Even if you don't need the air in your new living room circulated this way, paint the Casablanca a color appropriate to its surroundings, put a paper globe shade over the light fixture, and you're in.

Low-hanging lamps of other types that expose a ratty-looking length of electric cord can be wrapped with wide velvet ribbon. Finishing the wrapping off with a wide bow is a playful decorative touch.

Access between rooms of your new apartment or house may be improved by the simple expedient of removing a door or two. Light can be let into a dark room by replacing a solid door with one made of glass or Plexiglass panels. Privacy behind such a door can be restored by pulling down a window shade over the transparent part. If you want to keep guests in your dining room from seeing what magic you're up to in the kitchen, but hesitate to do anything to reduce ventilation, why not install a swinging door over part of the aperture between rooms? You know, the kind you see at the entrance to the saloon in movie westerns; it's usually made of wooden blinds.

Whatever you do about doors to the outside, don't let any realtor or builder convince you that the presence of a Dutch door (that's a door divided in half across its width about midway) adds to the value of the house. The Dutch door, originally made to let air in while keeping small animals out, is an affectation without any real living value today, at least not in my part of the world, where there are about three days in springtime when you want the outer door partly open before you definitely need a full-length screen door. I've lived in two different houses in the countryside that were "sold" to me as "full of charm" because of that dratted divided door to the back porch; I never once had such a door half open and half closed, which is supposed to be the point of it all!

I can see, however, that the application of a Dutch door to the bedroom of a small child might turn that room into a super playpen. With top open you could keep an ear out for baby from another room; yet, if he wakes and crawls about on the floor, with bottom half closed, he can't come in your room and get you up.

The improvement of the look of a door, exterior or interior, can sometimes be affected by replacing the hardware: wrought-iron bar hinges, for example, instead of the usual brass bolt-and-groove type, may complement your colonial furniture better. Or, gluing or nailing a "panel" of picture molding to a flush door lends the appearance of an earlier decade.

This brings us, once again, to the happy subject of windows, on which entire books have been written and doubtless will again be. Why not, since they are such a vital part of architecture *and* of interior decoration? Indeed a large dramatic window can become the focal point of a room's decor. One hopes, in that case, that what is seen through the window is a pleasant and soothing vista—not the wall across the air shaft, your neighbor's frantic supper preparations, or a series of trucks and mopeds whizzing by. If your "picture window" offers you one of the last-mentioned scenes, the best thing for you to do is brick or board it up as our colonial forebears did when they realized that they could reduce their real estate taxes that way. If you need the window for light and ventilation, it's possible that you can protect your privacy and peace of mind by obscuring only the bottom half. That's how cafe curtains were born. An innovative use of cafe curtains, by the way, is to hang the lower rod at window-sill level and "drape" the wall below the window to the floor with one set, while the top set of curtains drapes the whole window in the conventional way.

There's no rule, as far as I know, against painting the glass on the bottom half of your window, or blotting out unwelcome scenes with decals or contact paper, solid or in designs. Depend, then, on the upper half window for light and air.

The good old pull-down window shade, which has been protecting the privacy of city people for generations, is still one of the best means

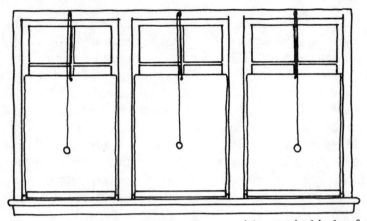

of keeping out the light or Peeping Toms, with certain kinds of windows. You can improve the standard shade provided by the usual landlord in any number of ways: paint or dye it, wallpaper it in part or whole, even glue fabric onto it to match some other aspect of your total decorative scheme. The standard window shade, by the way, doesn't *have* to pull down. It can be mounted at the bottom of the window and pull up. A hook at the window's top frame and a long string and curtain pull will do the job. A bank of several window sections might be attractively decorated by a different colored pull-up window shade in each panel, the hues reiterating colors used in the rest of the room.

I, personally, am devoted to slatted blinds, or louvres, and am most enthusiastic about this treatment for windows, either inside or outside the house. Slatted blinds on its windows the same color as the rest of the room's woodwork can "make" an otherwise dreary bedroom. Blinds or louvres don't fade or shred with time, you can hang things from them, and they need no tying back or hardware systems for drawing or pulling back.

Too often curtains on a pull-back track dictate the necessity for some sort of valance to be custom constructed at a prohibitive cost to the unhandy. If this shoe fits you, you can save some money by getting a valance made from cheap, unfinished wood and finishing it yourself. Sand and oil or wax it yourself, or paint it the same shade as your walls. Or cover it with fabric by the wielding of a hammer and some nails or a staple gun. The fabric needn't be the same as the drapes that will go under it. Perhaps it will be the leftover pieces from the slipcover you made for the armchair or the bedspread you fashioned from remnants. Pick up an old paisley shawl in a junk shop and cover the valance with that. Or simulate a solid valance by hanging scallop-edged, stiff fabric from a U-shaped curtain rod.

Venetian blinds, matchstick roll-up blinds, and related kinds that allow you to control the amount of light or air admitted have the added value of also decorating the room with patterns of light. You can also cast lovely shadow patterns by covering a too-small window with an old picture frame into which you have inserted a piece of clear plastic or Plexiglass. Scotch tape or glue onto the back of the transparent surface your collection of leaves, weeds, pressed flowers, fern fronds, moths, or what have you; let the light from the window pro-

ject this natural design onto other walls as the sun moves in its orbit. It makes an inexpensive and arresting decorative "mobile."

Here are some other treatments to bear in mind as you study ways to improve the appearance of the "eyes" of your home:

panels of wooden filigree work in front of the glass;

panels of fabric caught on rods top and bottom;

a flower box blooming with geraniums (inside, in winter) on windowsill or under the window;

a fringe of thick yarn looped over a rod at window top, falling free and knotted or tasseled at the bottom;

ribbon or string "woven" across window through nails or brads pounded into all sides of the window frame.

Nasty little high-up windows, like those in some basement apartments or ranch house bedrooms, are best improved by bringing them down, in effect, into the lower part of the room. Tall wooden frames with a sheer fabric stapled to their backs are good for this; so is a "fence" of bamboo or other similar reeds wedged between ceiling and floor surfaces across the window wall.

In the last analysis, however, a window well placed, nicely shaped, and in a pleasing relationship to the rest of the room's architecture, is often its own best "decoration." Keep frame and sill and panes (and dividers, if any), sparkling clean and whole; don't try to dress it up in any other way. Let the air and light that come through be the room's improvement. And, if inspiring sounds, smells, and sights are also to be let in, you've got it made.

Tips

- *If you rearrange furniture and find crush marks on the rug made by heavy pieces sitting too long in the same place, "repair" by putting a damp cloth over the marks and then pressing lightly with a warm (not hot) iron. Then fluff up the spots with your fingernail or a comb.*

- *People hesitate over installing venetian blinds, louvres, or slatted roll-ups because of the cleaning problem. Dusting a 9-foot venetian is no picnic, it's true; but, if you keep an old pair of cotton gloves for just this purpose alone, washing them out between dustings, you can make shorter work of it. Just use your gloved fingers for dusting each separate segment.*

- *Should your immediate neighborhood lack a lumberyard or wholesale wood dealer, you can buy molding by the foot at a framing shop.*
- *There are rug companies that sell carpeting for indecently low prices if you save up your old woolen coats and suits and send them to the company. Reversible rugs of recycled wool, such as those that were once made by the Olson Company, wear eternally. Consult the* Yellow Pages.

9

The Studio Apartment and Other All-Purpose Rooms

In England what's called a "bed-sitter" is more often known in the United States as a "studio apartment." No matter how you slice it, the one-room-for-all-purposes presents peculiar problems to the amateur decorator, as does the pullman or galley kitchen that is so frequently a part of this particular architectural manifestation. Lavish entertaining at home is another troublesome area for the small-studio dweller: taking any dinner party group over four to a nearby restaurant is the rule for meeting social obligations of this kind. And the dear Lord knows you can rapidly go broke this way. In the large studio apartment there is some leeway in the guest list limitation because the more spacious habitat is usually equipped with a dining table that grows for special occasions.

In any size studio apartment one of the secrets of success is multifunctional furniture, whether collapsible, expandable, or both—or neither. Some contemporary pieces that do everything but figure out your income tax are very beautiful indeed; surprisingly enough, unless custom-made they aren't all horrendously expensive. Part of the modern look is streamlining and simplicity, which make you think you have more space than you actually do. This look is also most restful to the eye.

Convertible sofas, which become beds when it's bedtime, are, of course, the prototype of multifunctional furniture; but they aren't the only sensible convertibles. The Scandinavians (and, less noticeably, the Italians, French, and Americans, too) make very good-looking, high-back lounge chairs that flip open in a second to become single beds. *You* can make an ottoman that does the same thing in a jiffy. Well, a few jiffies. Here's how.

How to Make a Convertible Ottoman–Bed

Materials and Tools Needed:
5 yards (approximately) of 36-inch upholstery fabric
three 26-inch lengths of 2-inch upholsterer's tape to match the fabric
three 27-inch zippers
needle and thread (or sewing machine)
4 pieces of foam rubber, each 4 1/2 × 24 × 24 inches

Directions:
1. Cut eight 26-inch squares out of the upholstery fabric, working from one selvage edge. These pieces will cover the flat sides of the cushions.
2. Cut from the fabric remaining four strips, 6 1/2 by 98 inches each. These lengths (some of which you may need to piece) will cover the sides of the cushions.
3. For the first cushion, stitch one 24-inch square of fabric to the border strip, edge to edge, wrong side out, making a 1-inch seam and taking great care turning the corners.
4. Now stitch the free edge of the side panel to another 24-inch square in the same way, but leaving one 24-inch edge plus 3 inches around the corner unjoined.
5. Insert one of the zippers into this opening and stitch it into place.
6. Repeat steps 3 through 5 for the other three cushions.
7. Turn cushion covers right side out.
8. Join them together by stitching upholsterer's tape first to one cushion cover and then to another. Be sure to make the three tape joinings at the correct edges, so that the cushions will pile up into a formation like a four-decker sandwich. See the illustration.
9. Force the foam rubber inside the cushion covers and work the corners into position.
10. Close the zippers and your ottoman-into-bed is completed.

This hassock, or ottoman, 18 inches high when not being sat upon, opens up into a mattress that is 2 by 8 feet. It's very simple to make, particularly since this kind of construction maintains a neater appearance of fit without any welting at its seams. Though the work will proceed faster with a sewing machine, you don't absolutely need one to make this ottoman; in fact, step 8 is better accomplished by hand

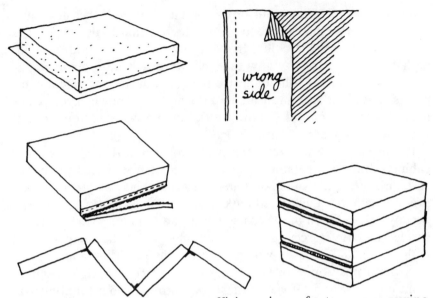

sewing, unless you have a more efficient zipper foot on your sewing machine than I have!

Making two of these four-cushion ottomans would relieve you of the necessity of buying a convertible Castro or Sealy, thus freeing your limited space for all sorts of other interesting furnishings. Actually, I have nothing personal against the convertible sofa except its enormous weight, which makes it impossible for me to pick one up off the sidewalk and bring it home with me when I see it abandoned there. If you think one of these gargantuas will answer your needs, you will save up to 75 percent of the original price by purchasing it on sale or secondhand. Watch the ads, including classifieds, in your local newspaper.

Scale is important in the one-room apartment; there should not be great disparity in the sizes and heft of articles of furniture. Nor should there be a boring lineup of all the bulky or heavy items on one side of the room. See Chapter 6 for more hints on how to create the illusion of balance where it's impossible to achieve in fact.

To make one room look like four, you must have pieces that are not too characteristically "bedroomy" or "denlike." Aside from a convertible sofa or the hassock just mentioned, a high-rise studio couch or a modified platform bed, with or without storage drawers underneath, will do it for the bed. But, in the middle of a two-by-four bed-sitter, an elaborate four-poster or curlicue brass bedstead just won't do. Better, far better, to go for the bed that folds up into the wall. Remember good old Mr. Murphy and his invention? You'll perhaps be surprised to know that the Murphy bed, or a contemporary version of it, is still going strong in certain city apartment complexes. The bed that disappears into the architecture when you're not using it remains one of the most efficient space-savers in existence. Don't dismiss it out of hand.

If you have one uninterrupted wall, cover it with shelves and/or cabinets and/or cube storage units, rather than sticking little bookcases, cabinets, and sound-system units around here and there, which produces a harried, cluttered look. Rather than a huge kneehole desk occupying too much of the space that is at a premium, gain a writing surface or built-in secretary by equipping one of the shelving units with a door that opens down on chains or metal folding brackets to a horizontal position. Voilà—writing desk. Place a straight chair in front of this section of wall unit, facing into the room for conversation when the "desk" is folded up. This way you have bought some floor space in the room for your dining table, armchairs, sofa, or whatever.

Conventional end tables in the studio situation are taboo. Make them count as something else as well: two-drawer cubes do this, as does a small table on wheels with an open shelf underneath. In the olden days of my childhood such an object was called a tea cart. To-

day, I believe the more usual label is "movable bar"; call it a gliding refreshment stand if you wish. Whatever its name, this piece of furniture is a good bet for a diminutive living space. Salton makes one with a keep-things-hot top shelf. Drop leaves on a cart-on-wheels make it instantly convertible into a fair-sized dining table.

In the very small one-room apartment a traditional dining table may be out. Even the table that converts into work desk when not being eaten from is de trop. Why not investigate other traditions of dining, such as the very low table with seating on pillows on the floor? This method, prevalent in some Asian countries, is a splendid custom that has the added advantage of keeping one limber into the later years. Many Western-world urban cliff dwellers have found it fits both their life-styles and their studio apartments. In a Sears showroom not long ago, I saw a version of this type of dining table, which would make supreme sense in the middle of a room where space is at a premium. It was a square wooden table, about 16 inches from the floor, with a cross-shaped pedestal underneath. The pedestal formed four equal cubical spaces under the table, into each one of which was stashed an exactly fitting wooden cube stool with a cushioned top—a coffee table when all the pieces are fitted together; a dining table for four when the stools or benches are pulled out. This sort of table would be very easy for the do-it-yourself carpenter to make, as would the seats. This is one project for which it would make sense to treat yourself to a really beautiful piece of solid wood, forsaking the ubiquitous plyboard for the tabletop. The grain of the wood could be a focal point of interest in your room.

How to Make a Wooden Coffee Table

Materials and Tools Needed:
one well-grained piece of 1-inch solid wood, 26 × 26 inches
two 3/4-inch plyboards, each 15 × 24 inches
four 15-inch lengths of 1-inch edging board
pad saw
woodworker's glue
rasp and sandpaper
oil and wax for finishing
four small L-shaped corner braces with screws to match

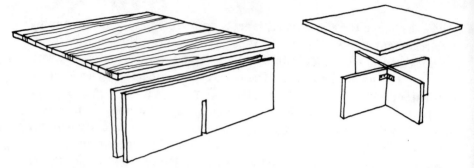

Directions:

1. On one 3/4-inch plyboard, mark a point 7 inches from the corner on the edge of one long side.
2. From this mark draw a 6-inch line across the board at right angles to the edge.
3. Draw another 6-inch line parallel to the first 1 inch from it. (The space between the lines should be in the exact center of the board's length.)
4. Repeat steps 1 through 3 on the other 3/4-inch plyboard.
5. Remove the section of plywood between the lines on each board.
6. Assemble the pedestal by putting the two plyboards together in cross shape by applying groove-to-groove.
7. Reinforce the pedestal by screwing in the corner braces close to the edge of the pedestal that will connect with the tabletop.
8. Glue the edging boards to the four outer edges of the cross and let the glue harden for several hours.
9. With a rasp and sandpaper smooth the corners and edges of the tabletop board.
10. Apply glue to the top of the pedestal and position the tabletop on it. Add weights along the location of the pedestal and allow glue to harden overnight.
11. Finish the tabletop and sides of edging board with oil and wax.

How to Make a Bench to Fit Under the Table

Materials and Tools Needed:
three pieces of 1/2-inch plywood or scrapwood, each 14 × 12 inches
two pieces of 1/2-inch plywood or scrapwood, each 14 × 11 inches
woodworker's glue
hammer and nails

one piece of 1/2-inch foam rubber, 14 × 12 inches
fabric to cover the seat
staple gun or upholstery tacks

Directions:
1. One of the first three pieces of plywood is your bench top; cover it with the foam and then the fabric by stapling or nailing the fabric all around the underside of the board.
2. Assemble the box frame by gluing the four remaining boards together, the longer two overlapping the shorter two at the corners. Allow glue to dry for several hours.
3. Reinforce this frame with a few nails at the corners (or, optionally, corner braces like the ones used in the table project, applied *inside* the box frame).
4. Glue the seat board, fabric side up, to the top of the frame and allow glue to harden overnight.

Now, unless you wish to finish the wood surfaces by staining or painting, one of your seating benches is finished. Multiply this easy construction by four and you have the whole dining unit.

A variation on these seat boxes—hinging the top and providing them with bottoms—would increase their usefulness; the cubes would then have acquired storage space inside, an important consideration for the undercloseted, small studio.

The folding table is an arch space-saver, whether round, pie-topped, or the 30-inch-square standard card table form. Such a table constitutes instant dining-for-one, all by itself, particularly if accompanied by a folding chair. How the fold-up table fits into the multi-functional scheme of things is as follows: unless you have closet space to accommodate it inconspicuously, choose a folding table with a

handsome top surface. Inlaid wood-patterned composition; checkerboard plastic tiles; well-grained veneer—folding tables come with these and many other decorative tops. When it's folded up, let the table function as a fireplace screen or wall covering. A folding table that is simply a splash of solid color in a shade that is your principal accent can serve to give unity to your decoration scheme.

File cases that are also pedestals for a desk or tabletop are an example of doubling up. So is multiple seating that is also storage space, as with a long settle bench whose seat is a lift-up lid. Rather than four individual boxes as outlined in the project above, make two long benches out of crate wood, cover with foam-and-fabric cushions for seat softening, put them against a wall—or in an L-shape with one at right angles to the wall—and you've solved another space problem.

Room dividers in a small studio apartment can be of the hang-a-curtain-from-the-ceiling type, or they can be pieces of furniture themselves. A floor-to-ceiling bookcase with a solid back can separate the living-room–study area from the sleeping room, the solid back either functioning as a headboard or providing a bedroom wall with nothing against it. The same tall bookcase, even if it doesn't quite reach the ceiling, can separate living room from dining area by having a table against its solid back. A refinement of this mode is to attach a drop leaf to the back of the bookcase unit, thereby saving room: a corridor when the leaf is folded down, a dining room when it's lifted into position. Folding legs under the tabletop complete the arrangement.

Accordian-type plastic on a ceiling drapery channel can separate nursery from adult living space if you have a baby while living in a studio apartment. Or you can create a bedroom for a suddenly inherited teenager by wood-paneling blinds that accordian back against the wall when you need to extend the main room again. In your diminutive studio room, however, you may not want to sacrifice even the space that something piling up in an accordian-pleated way necessitates. In that case, your best bet is something very narrow hanging from the ceiling or rising from the floor. Stretch an attractive piece of batik or a hand-hooked or needlepoint mat between two spring-tension poles that go from floor to ceiling. Wind around the poles yards and yards of machine-embroidered edging you picked up for pennies at a remnant shop, filling in the space between.

If the illusion of division (rather than absolute privacy) is acceptable, divide a room with old window screens hung from the ceiling. Window screens can be painted—frames, wire mesh, and all—to blend with the color of your walls or ceiling. Paint the wire portions, one side at a time, allowing for drying in between, by using a sponge and backing the nonaction side with newspaper or cardboard. Or divide your room with a roll-up blind or window shade with a "wall" of tall plants coming up from window boxes on the floor, or with hanging plant holders at different levels.

Recently, in the furniture department of one of the world's largest department stores I saw this: a very efficient looking room divider made of large, heavy, oblong wooden frames, filled with heavy canvas panels that were edged with grommets. Through the grommets was strung stout rope, which held the panels in place inside the frames. It looked like nothing so much as a group of trampolines on their ends; and its price was astronomical. The point of all this? It reminded me to advise you that if you've moved into a small studio apartment because of the rising cost of upkeep on your yacht, now, at least, you can get some use out of your old sails. When they're no longer seaworthy, use the sails for a room divider. Hang them from a track in the ceiling.

A high-backed sofa, whether convertible or not, can function as a room divider of the more modified type; place the sofa in the middle of the room, not backed against a wall. So, of course, can shelf-and-cabinet units, whether they go clear to the ceiling or not. If not, be sure they are substantial enough not to tip easily.

Since the studio apartment is usually a temporary arrangement—

not many tenants sign forty year leases to move into one—strenu-
ously built-in furniture is not a good plan. Also, you may decide to
move your furniture around by whim or seasonal dictate. If you think
either of these cases fits you, then obviously you opt for the movable
room divider, such as a spring-pole arrangement. Putting shelf or
cabinet units on wheels ensures easy movability. Here come again the
roller skates or casters mentioned in Chapter 7.

Kitchen facilities that accompany all-purpose rooms are usually
not on the grand scale. If the kitchen is really only one corner of your
room, you might consider separating it off with some sort of island-
counter-and-barstool arrangement—another multifunctional furnishing unit. There are other things you can do to capitalize on the
kitchen work area, too. The compact range-atop-refrigerator fixture
saves a lot of breathing space. You may be using up precious refrigerator space unnecessarily with things like pickles and chutneys, jams
and jellies, dried or smoked fish, onions and eggs, all of which can
live very well outside refrigeration for long or short periods of time.
For example, I just now removed from my fridge two jars of pickled
chili beans left behind by the previous owner of my house. Chilies *are*
a preservative; they don't require the aid of near-freezing tempera-
tures. By this act I made available a whole new bunch of space for
more perishable items.

If your food preparation area lacks sufficient work surface near the
stove, you will want to use the sink for that: just cover it with a breadboard, or piece of butcher block, or any good cutting or kneading surface. You can extend counter space that way when the water is not
running. Often around building sites you can find good pieces of formica-topped wood cutouts that serve this purpose very well. These
planks are the holes that builders have cut out of formica topping
around sinks, so it's right that they should be used by the penny-
pinching decorator for covering a (somewhat smaller) sink. For storing, they slide into spaces that accommodate a tray. The big cut-rate
department store near me advertises from time to time something
called an "over-the-sink cutting board." It's only about 2 dollars when
it's on special; but there's no need for you to shoot even this small sum
when you can pick one up for free.

A handsome and efficient freezer-to-stove-top-to-table covered
casserole or Dutch oven is a must for the studio apartment dweller.
Cast iron, with or without enamel outer layer, gets my vote for even

cooking, durability, and decorative beauty, too. Other items connected with preparing, serving, and eating meals should, for the studio denizen, be multifunctional and kept to a minimum. You can't fit six sets of chinaware or 200 pounds of sterling silver flatware into most one-roomers I've seen!

One room can be divided into two or three by giving it different floor levels. A simple platform in one corner suggests stepping up to boudoir or dining room. Sleeping lofts are really easy to make yourself, though you may prefer to do your sleeping on basic level and put your study or dining area up on high. A bowerlike arrangement, with a mattress on top and table and chairs underneath is not bad, and a simple carpentry problem. Modifications of the bunk bed project in Chapter 5 could do it. So could two-by-fours upright, supporting a platform and a ladder. Climbing up to perform some living function is a good way not to waste that space at the top of an apartment that has limited floor space, but high ceilings.

You can also suggest a division into three rooms by how you treat the floor. Where the carpet begins is where you step from dining room into parlor or the edge of the vinyl tile can provide demarcation between kitchen and living–sleeping room.

The glass-top table finds its place more often in the modest one-room apartment than in its original home—a huge patio. It creates the illusion of a more spacious room, as do any furniture pieces you can see through, such as cane-back chairs, metal filigree shelves, ladderback chairs, or seating with backs of lateral bands of fabric or leather. This is true for couches, chairs, or cabinets that you can see under. They give off a more commodious, airy feeling than those that go solidly down to the floor all around.

If your room dividing by construction is restricted to building a foot-high platform, you may want to get extra mileage out of the platform by hiding a mattress on a wooden board underneath. Put the mattress support on rollers and pull it out at night; even twin beds can be done this way. You now have sitting room, study, or dining area on top, bedroom stuffed beneath.

A word about pattern and color in the one-room apartment: the simpler and fewer, the better. Solid colors in most wall, ceiling, and floor coverings allow you to use some pattern in fabrics. They also provide a better background for a "busy" painting or print, a heavily textured area rug, a complicated chandelier. If you force more than

one figured fabric plus one stripe or geometric pattern into a small room, you will reduce the illusion of space and serenity. Lighter tones in ceilings and walls will push them out a bit, make you think there's a bit more room than in fact there is. Dark floors *and* walls *and* ceilings in a studio apartment may produce a feeling of claustrophobia. Leave the purple, ebony, and chocolate brown in the accents, rather than the architectural elements and larger pieces of furniture. White latex paint over that mahogany bookcase—bone walls; eggshell carpeting; wheat-color ceiling. It may sound like dullsville to you, but when you splash in those persimmon sofa pillows, lime-green drapery, that black-topped, shiny lacquered table, and the flowered cretonne spread your mother gave you for a going away present, you'll be glad you stayed with the soft, neutral shades as background.

Matching wall covering and curtain (or upholstery) fabrics are a boon to the one-room dweller, a development that your grandmother wasn't able to avail herself of. A multicolor figured pattern in wallpaper, drapes, and slipcovers, even in one far-from-large room, isn't necessarily a disaster, especially if other decoration is of a more subdued order in form and color.

The studio apartment is the place to use one accessory where people with more ample dwelling space would use two. This is a good penny-pinching tenet, too, since pairs of things reduced by circumstance to singles are always cheaper to buy in secondhand shops, at auctions, at flea markets, and at garage sales. One graceful andiron makes a pleasant corner filler. A sturdy wooden gate post can become a tall plant holder or a pedestal for a table. Bookends or candlesticks, when solo, still function as they were meant to notwithstanding the loss of a mate. The one exception may be antique carriage lanterns— singles bring pretty fancy prices, but that's because of their reverend age. All bets are off when you get into the realm of true antiques.

My parents once found at a tremendous bargain in a country auction an antique carriage lantern that had already been affixed to an iron post. Trembling with excitement, they brought it home to their retirement cottage, a small house at the end of a long, straight driveway. The only trouble was that they could never agree *where* the lantern should be erected, my father claiming it would be best at the street end of the driveway, my mother holding out for level with the corner of the house. Hence, the lantern never did get put up; it moved to another state with them and was eventually sold to an antique dealer in the new location.

Living in a one-room flat sometimes becomes more attractive when one realizes that he has considerable advantages not enjoyed by the many-rooms dweller. Prime among these is that the whole furnishing allowance can be concentrated on one or two good pieces of furniture or decoration. Let the word *good* predominate; an investment in a piece of real junk, whether found at a champagne price in a fancy antique shop or commissioned to be built for you, is no investment at all. Take your time, comparison shop, learn the hallmarks of quality in whatever item you're shopping for. And choose a rug, convertible sofa, pair of chairs, desk–table, watercolor, or piece of sculpture that will please you for years to come.

Tips

- *Use scraps of fabric left over from slip-covering or upholstering to mat prints with, or photographs. Hanging on the wall, they will act as a decorative coordinator.*
- *Cup hooks and other types of screws can be worked into nearly any type of surface without your having an electric drill and set of drill bits. Just select a nail that is a bit smaller in girth than the screw you want to put in. Pound the nail into the wood, wallboard, or whatever to slightly less depth than the length of the thread portion of the screw. Remove nail and put in screw with fingers and screwdriver. Even brick, if somewhat aged, will take a cup hook without crumbling.*
- *Never order paint blindly. It comes in so many variations of any one color that to phone up and ask the paint store to send you a quart of green paint is to invite an unloading of something too bilious to have moved off the shelves.*

10 A Compendium of Decorative Accessories That Need Never Be Bought—At Least Not in the Usual Places

Air Fresheners

If we concur that good smells are an essential part of a well-designed home, then we are in important agreement. Foodstuffs and cooking aromas provide them in kitchens and dining rooms; charcoal and burning wood can do it in a room that boasts a wood-burning stove or fireplace. Hanging up boughs of pine, balsam, and other softwoods at seasons other than Yuletide (like when the utilities workers have trimmed them off and left them by the side of the road) can improve the quality of your house air. And placing a cologne-soaked bit of surgical cotton on a sconce-type light bulb at night will disperse your favorite scent into the atmosphere of bath or bedroom for a little while.

Ashtrays

Anyone who buys one is off his rocker, since so many containers function so well this way. Just be sure that the inside finish can withstand a little heat. Seashells work very nicely in other than seaside cottages; terra-cotta flowerpot saucers are good, too. So are metal cough-drop boxes on which you've painted over the commercialism. Classiest of all are china saucers whose cup mates have long since disappeared.

Bar Tools

These can be borrowed from workshop or kitchen for the occasion, as they tend to be things like strainers, picks, tongs, and small mallets (or hammers). A perfect ice crusher is a wooden potato masher plus a small canvas bag.

Bookends

If you don't fancy a pair of rampant pewter lions or rearing glass horses, stones and shells can hold books together. Or to avoid the cliche of a pair of antique flatirons with a Peter Hunt design on them, why not two thrown-away, not-so-antique pressing irons you find in the dump?

Book or Manuscript Holders

A small lectern effect *is* handy in the kitchen or at the work desk. Keep your eyes open and you'll find just the right rack in the discarded metal department of the local landfill area. Mine, shaped like an A-type tent with steel ribs and a holding lip, works fine. I have no idea what its original function was.

Colored Glass Bottles

If you're an antique glass collector, you know that some of the gorgeous shades old bottles and jars were made in can hardly be duplicated today. You also doubtless realize that this hobby can reduce you to penury fast. If there is still some room on the window sill or sash for colored glass, you can achieve a similar effect by rescuing some nicely shaped liquor bottles from your neighborhood bar just before yon barkeeper starts smashing this week's accumulation of empties in a barrel. Take home your treasures, fill or half-fill them with water, and add a few drops of food coloring to each. The light shining through will do the rest.

Decanter Tops That Fit

One might find stray glass tops and one might pick up topless bottles and decanters, and, in my experience, anyway, never the twain shall meet. But the other day I made a perfect match by the simple expedient of hollowing out a cork jug stopple, fitting the too-skinny crystal bottle top into the cork, and fixing it with a bit of glue.

Decorative Pillows

Obviously, they can be made from any sort of stuffing: foam bits, rags, feathers, down, kapok, nylon hose, etc. And they can be covered with anything from last winter's apron to next summer's beach robe. Shape is what is challenging. If you want to create visual interest with pillows, don't adhere to the ordinary square or rectangle: try making pillows in circles, triangles, ice-cream cone shapes, and even hearts, flowers, and certain species of animals. I have one in the form of a lobster—not a bad conversation piece.

Doorstops

These are essential in windy houses that you want also to be quiet, restful homes. Handsome, small boulders are attractive used in this way. Or cover a brick with some bright scrap of soft fabric that won't scratch the floor. How about a small pail filled with sand, a stump of wood, a jug of stoneware, or a single andiron?

Dried Arrangements

Admittedly, this garnishment is easier for the country or small-town dweller to effect than the city kid. Besides the tall pampas grass mentioned in Chapter 6, I can gather within yards of my house milkweed, mullen, cattails, Joe-Pye weed, teasel, and a host of other plants that dry nicely and combine well. But don't sell short the city empty lot, where you can often find such good-lookers as dock, goldenrod, pigweed, timothy grass, and the occasional wild wand of wheat or oat. Finish drying them out in your oven, then bleach or color them for a fun look in a flower vase.

Fireplace Screens

Town dumps are full of stuff that can be used to keep the sparks from setting your house afire. So are the sidewalks of cities: discarded metal-edged window screens; grillwork from doors, gates, or fences; parts of dead stoves or refrigerators. Or stretch some guinea-pig wire around a couple of metal mop sticks. Or line up some metal-mesh ironing boards.

Hat Racks

Antlers from some poor beast set in mahogany around a mirror used to be the sine qua non; then it was a sturdy oak upright with metal hooks growing out of its sides. But how about planting a many-pronged hunk of driftwood from your beach wandering, or the shed limb of a fruitwood tree, in your front entryway and calling it sculpture? Who's to say you can't hang hats on it?

Pot Holders

So easily are pot holders made of old pieces of toweling with smooth fabric to cover that it's scarcely worth mentioning. If you decide to knit or crochet some, though, be sure to use several-ply yarn and line them, too, so your fingers won't come through onto a hot pot. Another choice is to use Baby's padded bibs when he's finished with them.

Jewelry Cases

If you don't care for the suggestion in Chapter 3, how about borrowing the small metal chest with the plastic drawers from the workshop—the one that holds tacks, nails, and such? Paint the metal to go with the colors of your bedroom. Or cover a cigar box with a scrap of your bedroom drapery fabric or paste cancelled stamps all over a cigarette or lozenge tin.

Lampshades

You can find any size or shape of lampshade frame you desire in a thrift shop or an incinerator room; then just stretch pillowcase fabric on it, sewing it fast to the bottom, top, and ribs of the frame. Or cut parchment in sections, punch holes in it, and thread it with yarn or plastic cord to the lampshade frame. One of the best-looking lampshades I ever made was done in cotton patchwork. Another—for a glass lamp chimney—was formerly a metal bowl with its bottom rusted out. Large, round, cardboard ice-cream cartons with a design punched in their sides make good lampshades, too.

Machinery Covers

Toaster, mixer, adding machine, typewriter, hair dryer, electric shaver, and any number of other domestic machines look delightfully mysterious (besides being kept dust-free) if you fashion sleeping-time covers for them out of leftover pieces of fabric that is used elsewhere in the room.

Mobile Sculptures

A marvelous way to purfle the space under your cathedral ceiling or over Baby's bed is to add a mobile. Using laundered-shirt cardboards, cut out flowers, beasts, or free-form shapes; water-color them in pleasant hues and suspend them on dark sewing-cotton threads. Or flatten some aluminum beverage cans and cut shapes out of the metal. You don't have to be Alexander Calder to work out some interestingly balanced moving parts, fastened to one another by thin wire.

Oriental Paintings

If you don't paint it yourself or have a friend who will lend you temperas in exchange for your displaying them on your walls, don't ever spend a month's salary on something that may not "wear well," especially if your taste tends to change with the years. Rent one instead from your museum or library and live with it for a while. If you really fall in love with it and want to keep it, you can probably buy it for a fraction of what you'd have spent at a gallery.

Oriental Rugs

These are priceless objects that withstand the test of time niftily. *Worn* ones (in some circles now the vogue) can be found in any secondhand shop for pennies or at town dump for free. You should never buy a new one, anyway, because it only encourages cruel child labor. (Did you realize that the fibers are all hand-tied by little children, who have to "retire" from this occupation at about age nine, when their fingers have grown too large to perform efficiently any more? Or is this a calumny?)

Paperweights

Those glass globules with bubbles or colorful designs inside are swell, but collectors' items now. Stones and shells (again), bits of metal and chrome of fascinating shape—the sort of thing shed by automobiles and found lying in the streets—do admirably, as do fascinatingly shaped metal attachments for ancient sewing machines. My paper-weights are whatever solid items are found in the vicinity of paper that needs holding down plus a collection of huge bolts (a friend de-rusted and nickel-coated them), which were picked up while I was walking a disused railroad track.

Pincushions

Remember those little strawberry-shaped sharpeners we used to find in our mothers' sewing baskets? All they are is fine sand inside a small cotton sack. Why not make a pincushion by finding a tiny basket or box—or a teacup with a missing handle—then sewing up a little pil-low in the contours of the inside of the container out of pretty cotton from the patchwork bag? Stuff your completed sack roundly with sand, uncooked rice, dried beans, or balsam and cedar needles to a fine plumpness. Close the opening with a few stitches.

Plant Pots

If, by now, you've used up all your plain terra-cotta pots by turning them into lamps, cake cookers, toilet paper holders, and other ac-cessories, you may have to knock together some pots for your plants out of scrap wood. Line them with tin foil or plastic sheeting and the moisture from the soil won't spoil your wood surfaces. Or put plants into cuspidors (the old yankees used to call them, frankly, spit-toons!), which have a pleasing conformation.

Rolling Plant Stands

For a heavy plant that wants to roll from winter sun window to sum-mer light or swing with your redecoration you need a rolling stand—a favorite of the mail-order houses. Save yourself about 15 dollars by attaching your child's outgrown roller skates to a slab of scrap wood or plywood, whose edges you can line with metal sold by hardware stores (for lining the edges of furniture like kitchen counters).

Serving Trays

The cork bulletin board you've brought home from the office, if you haven't mounted a picture on it, will serve drinks to guests effectively. So will any old board from a child's game, if it has a raised edge and is made of some nonslippery material. Turn the game board over and look on the underside to be sure.

Tablecloths for Round Table

I beg to remind you that tablecloths don't have to be all one piece and bought for an outrageous price. Use an old sheet or bedspread cut up into semicircles or quadrants. Then sew them together into a large circle.

Tea Cozies

You know that little quilted cover that keeps the teapot warm while you gossip over a cuppa. I find that a knitted wool cap a friend discarded as not any longer fashionable does this job very well and looks perky, too.

Tie-Backs

If not of the same material as your curtains, these could be lengths of light chain, silk cord, grosgrain ribbon, ladies' belts, gaily colored yarn or string, binding tape, the elasticized waistbands of the old worn-out panty hose you have braided into a rug or place mat, or men's or women's garters.

Umbrella Stands

You can lose an arm and a leg purchasing one of these in antique American wood or Chinese porcelain. But a plain, old, rough ceramic birdbath that long ago lost its flat-dish top is a good umbrella stand. Just put a small metal or plastic dish with a sponge in it under the hollow column. Or use the remains of a rusted-out, metal, round, gas space-heater; or use a heating duct based in a block of cork.

Wall Clocks

If you have smashed the glass and lost the numerals of your Big Ben and it still keeps Greenwich time, you can turn the works into a decorative wall clock. Pick up a piece of thin wood with a knothole in it for the hands to come through. Then crayon or paint the hours on the face or make them with thumbtacks, upholstery tacks, or paper fasteners. Hang your new clock on the wall. If the hands don't seem long enough to you, glue Popsicle sticks or drinking straws to the existing hands.

I just now made a "kitcheny" clock for my skullery wall by doing the above, except that in place of the thin slab of wood, I used the plastic bottom of a weighted pet-feeding dish that had fallen apart. Since I have no electric drill, I punched the hole in the middle with an ice pick, an indispensable instrument for the amateur decorator.

Wine or Water Carafes

Cut glass or Steuben ware is peachy—if you inherited one. If not, buy a bottle of Paul Masson wine. The beverage may not be beloved of Alex Lichine, but the container it comes in is a masterpiece of good design. I once found such a bottle in a moving-out neighbor's trash can, perhaps because of an ugly scratch or acid stain down the side. I quickly covered the imperfection with a length of bright green banana tape and pressed the bottle into service as a cut-flower vase.

Wine Cellars

Easily made by picking up from a building site a few earthenware drainage or flue cylinders. Build a pyramid of these perfect-size tubes; only the base row must be braced to keep them from rolling apart. The rest will stay in place through shape and texture.

Wind Machines

Charming sounds are certainly part of the atmosphere of a well-decorated house. Aside from bird sounds outside and recorded music inside, I enjoy a harmonicalike melody through one window every time the wind cracks its cheeks. You can make your own wind machine from discarded microscope slides or old brass curtain-rod sections, cosmetics tubes, or fountain pen cylinders. Or use a piece of bamboo, such as a segmented leg from a defunct étagère. Suspend these items in a circle through a plastic can cover and hang the whole thing up in a draft.

Index